Guide to
Caravan and Camping
Holidays

COLOUR

GW00501483

Newquay
Holiday Parks

are great!

For families and couples, young and old.

Choose from three Parks all with the highest standard facilities, excellent services and great, great value for money.

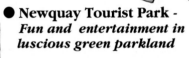

- **Newquay Tourist Park** - *Fun and entertainment in luscious green parkland*
- **Holywell Bay Holiday Park** - *next to a sandy, family beach*
- **Crantock Beach Holiday Park** - *with lovely sea views in a peaceful setting*

Great choice ● Great locations ● Great fun!

Phone for a colour brochure now!
(0637) 871111

Please ask for extension 15

Newquay Holiday Parks Ltd, 15 Newquay Tourist Park, Newquay, Cornwall TR8 4HS

FAMILY HOLIDAYS IN
CORNWALL

ON THE BEACH

ST. IVES BAY HOLIDAY PARK

With PANORAMIC VIEWS and private access to three miles of sandy beach. A Choice of licenced premises. FREE entertainment. Childrens rooms and playgrounds. Indoor heated POOL. Supermarket. Laundrette, hire shop. Pets Welcome.

CHALETS - Sleeping 2/4/5/6 persons Luxury to budget. All electric with fridge, toilet, bath. colour TV.

CARAVANS - Sleeping 2/3/4/5/6/8 Flush toilet. Electricity. TV. Most with showers & fridges.

CAMPING - Bookable pitches, electric hookups. Sea views. Casuals welcome. All Sanitary facilities (including hot water.)

Mr O. White   Tel: 0736 752274 (24 Hour Service)
ST. IVES BAY HOLIDAY PARK,
Upton Towans, Hayle, Cornwall TR27 5BH

Name _____

Address _____
BLOCK CAPITALS PLEASE
_____
_____

PLEASE FORWARD **FREE** COLOUR BROCHURE & TERMS   **OW**

Dorset

"Happy Holidays" by the sea at
FRESHWATER HOLIDAY PARK

A family site with large Camping and Touring field
- Caravans for hire • Own private beach
- Heated swimming pools • Club complex
- Entertainment nightly (Whitsun - mid September)
- Licensed restaurant • Supermarket • Amusements
- Take-away • Free hot showers • Launderette
- Horse/Pony rides • Golf course adjoining site
- Fine country and Seaside walks • Caravan sales

Colour brochure from Mr F. A. Coads
FRESHWATER HOLIDAY PARK
Burton Bradstock
Near Bridport Dorset DT6 4PT
Telephone: (0308) 897317
Fax: (0308) 897336

BIG, BEAUTIFUL 55 ACRE PARK

2 HEATED INDOOR & OUTDOOR SWIMMING POOLS

CHILDREN'S ADVENTURE PLAYGROUND

ENTERTAINMENTS

BMX TRACK

LICENSED CLUBHOUSE

TEEN'S DISCO

SOLARIUM

MINI GYM & SAUNA

CRAZY GOLF

HORSE RIDING

PONY TREKKING

STABLES

BIKE HIRE

FISHING NEARBY

FOREST WALKS

LAUNDERETTE

GENERAL STORE

BARBECUE

CAFETERIA & TAKEAWAY

PRE-BOOKABLE TOURING & TENT PITCHES

ERVICE PLOTS WITH PLUG-IN MAINS ELECTRIC & WATER

LSO STATIC HOLIDAY HOMES FOR SALE. ASK FOR DETAILS

(SOME FACILITIES ONLY VAILABLE AT PEAK TIMES)

A HOLIDAY FOR ALL THE FAMILY

It's not easy finding a holiday all the family will love, whatever their age, whatever their interests... so relax, you've just found it! A Village Holiday offers all-weather fun, excitement and well earned relaxation for mum, dad and the kids–even gran and grandpa! This 55 acre, well equipped caravan /camping park is positioned in beautiful forest surroundings only 8 miles from Bournemouth.

£100 FREE
ENTERTAINMENT VOUCHERS
with each 7 day holiday
booking

at Oakdene

I enclose S.A.E. for   full details ☐   off-peak bargains ☐   Please tick

Name _____

Address _____

_____

Village Holidays at Oakdene Holiday Park, Dept FHG94, St. Leonards, Ringwood, Hants BH24 2RZ. 24 hr Tele-brochure service: 0202 875422

Hampshire

TOURERS PARADISE

Our exclusive touring site at Lytton Lawn is arguably the best holiday location for caravan tourers in Britain. Only 2½ miles from Shorefield Country Park, Lytton Lawn is set in beautiful natural parkland close to Milford beach, which has spectacular views to the Isle of Wight. Three miles inland is the historic and unspoilt New Forest with its deer and wild ponies. Every conceivable leisure facility is on site or close by: sailing, fishing, horse-riding, golf, tennis and lots more. Caravans have individual pitches, with plenty of space for the car, caravan or tent, awning and barbecue.

All facilities are provided including:
- Electricity hook up ■ Childrens' play area
- Showers and purpose built launderette

Plus FREE Membership to the Shorefield Leisure Club:

- Indoor/outdoor pools
- Snooker lounge
- Sauna, solarium and jacuzzi
- Top class restaurant
- Dance studio
- Special facilities for children
- Nightly entertainment

- Rallies welcome

For a FREE BROCHURE phone
0590 642513 quoting GCC
Shorefield Country Park,
Shorefield Rd., Downton,
Nr. Lymington,
Hants SO41 0LH

WINNER
— 1990 —

SHOREFIELD COUNTRY PARK

C6   **Please mention Guide to Caravan and Camping Holidays when enquiring**

FOR THE MUTUAL GUIDANCE
OF GUEST AND HOST

Every year literally thousands of holidays, short-breaks and overnight stops are arranged through our
guides, the vast majority without any problems at all. In a handful of cases, however, difficulties do
arise about bookings, which often could have been prevented from the outset.

It is important to remember that when accommodation has been booked, both parties — guests
and hosts — have entered into a form of contract. We hope that the following points will provide
helpful guidance.

GUESTS: When enquiring about accommodation, be as precise as possible. Give exact dates,
numbers in your party and the ages of any children. State the number and type of rooms wanted and
also what catering you require — bed and breakfast, full board, etc. Make sure that the position about
evening meals is clear — and about pets, reductions for children or any other special points.

Read our reviews carefully to ensure that the proprietors you are going to contact can supply what
you want. Ask for a letter confirming all arrangements, if possible.

If you have to cancel, do so as soon as possible. Proprietors do have the right to retain deposits and
under certain circumstances to charge for cancelled holidays if adequate notice is not given and they
cannot re-let the accommodation.

HOSTS: Give details about your facilities and about any special conditions. Explain your deposit
system clearly and arrangements for cancellations, charges, etc, and whether or not your terms
include VAT.

If for any reason you are unable to fulfil an agreed booking without adequate notice, you may be
under an obligation to arrange alternative suitable accommodation or to make some form of
compensation.

While every effort is made to ensure accuracy, we regret that FHG Publications cannot accept
responsibility for errors, omissions or misrepresentation in our entries or any consequences thereof.
Prices in particular should be checked because we go to press early. We will follow up complaints
but cannot act as arbiters or agents for either party.

BEACH BUNGALOW
OUR WORLD BY THE SEA

Executive Beach Bungalow, in its own grounds, quiet secluded cove, with your own beach, moments from your Patio door. Every comfort in an area of outstanding natural beauty. On flat coastal strip with sub-tropical plants confirming Gulf Stream mild climate. Tour beautiful Snowdonia, 'The Castles' and the famous Llyn Peninsula and beaches. Tastefully furnished by Parker Knoll. Modern split level lounge-dining room, overlooking lawn, beach and sea. 3 bedrooms, vanitory units. TV's and duvets; 1 & 2 Double & Single; 3 Single or double; 4 children's upstairs 4 singles; 2 Bathrooms en-suite. Teletext colour TV' video, compact disc tape and music centre, dishwasher, microwave, fridge, freezer, washing machine, tumble dryer, electric blankets, telephone and central heating, patio furniture, parking 5 cars. P.O. and shop handy. Safe bathing and water sports, sea/river fishing. Nearby Restaurants, Bar Snacks, take-aways and most leisure activities, including golf, rambling, pony trekking, three modern Leisure Centres. Featured by BBC and Wales Tourist Board (top grade 5 award). Come and inspect any time, between Caernarfon and Nefyn on A499 (Llyn Peninsula). Try a £49 Minibreak.

JAN	FEB	MARCH	APRIL	MAY	JUNE	JULY	AUG	SEPT	OCT	NOV	DEC
1 - £109	5 - £99	5 - £139	2BH - £369	7 - £219	4 - £329	2 - £429	6 - £549	3 - £415	1 - £269	5 - £159	3 - £99
8 - £89	12 - £99	12 - £149	9 - £229	14 - £229	11 - £339	9 - £499	13 - £549	10 - £389	8 - £229	12 - £149	10 - £99
15 - £79	19 - £109	19 - £156	16 - £199	21 - £259	18 - £379	16 - £529	20 - £529	17 - £359	15 - £229	19 - £129	17 - £299
22 - £79	26 - £109	26 - £199	23 - £189	28BH - £429	25 - £389	23 - £549	27BH - £499	24 - £319	22 - £299	26 - £119	24 - £399
29 - £89			30MD - £199						29 - £249		31 - £259

Deposit ¼ of total. Minimum £50 p.w. and Insurance £3 nightly. Sleeps 10, over 5 persons £5 per night each.
Free electric allowance £7. Central Heating 70° £35 weekly. (Dogs £5 nightly, 2 only. Never left alone). Weekend, Midweek or Week Breaks Phone 0286 660400

VILLA CHALET

Your own beach, moments from your lounge patio sliding door, overlooking lawn, beach and sea. Every comfort, Lounge dinette, exclusive 3 piece suite. Teletext colour TV, Electric fire, bed settee, 3 separate bedrooms. 1 Double, vanitory basin, en-suite to bathroom, electric blankets and heater. 2 Double, or 2 singles, two drop-down beds for children. 3 Single with drop-down bed. Blankets and pillows provided. Bring linen, towels or own duvet? Kitchen area. Microwave, electric hob & oven, fridge-freezer, slow cooker, kettle, toaster and Hoover. Bathroom. Sit-down shower-bath, wash basin, toilet. Well heated, patio furniture, much up market Dragon Award. Featured by the BBC and Wales Tourist Board. View any time. Try a £25 Minibreak.

WALES *It's magic*

MARCH	APRIL	MAY	JUNE	JULY	AUGUST	SEPT	OCT
12 - £78	2BH - £178	7 - £158	4 - £238	2 - £278	6 - £328	3 - £268	1 - £148
19 - £98	9 - £128	14 - £178	11 - £248	9 - £288	13 - £328	10 - £228	8 - £128
26GF - £128	16 - £98	21 - £188	18 - £258	16 - £308	20 - £328	17 - £198	15 - £108
.	23 - £108	28BH - £318	25 - £268	23 - £308	27BH - £318	24 - £178	22 - £168
	30MD - £128			30 - £328			

New 2 Bedroomed, Similar, Deduct £25 from above rates. Deposit ¼ of total. Minimum £50 p.w. and Insurance £2 nightly. Sea view £3 nightly. Full Heating 70° £5 nightly. Limited to 8, over 5 persons £3 per night each. (Dogs, £3 nightly, never left alone, 2 only). Weekend, Midweek or Week Breaks Phone 0286 660400

BEACH HOLIDAY HOME

BEACH MODERN LUXURY HOLIDAY HOME (Tourist Board approved caravan)

Your own beach, moments from your door. Top Grade 5 award. 6-berth B type, 2 bedrooms: 8 berth A type, 2 bedrooms limited to 6: 10 berth A type, 3 bedrooms limited to 8. Lounge, Kitchen, Dinette, Bedrooms, 1st, one Double; 2nd, some have a Single with a drop-down Bed, or 2 Singles to make a Double; 3rd, Single or Twins, some make a Double. Request on phone and on white booking form. In some a Double Bed Settee makes up in the Lounge/Dinette. Blankets and pillows provided. Bring linen and towels or own duvet? Bathroom, shower, wash basin, toilet. Well heated, remote control Colour TV, Fridge, Large Cooker, Electric Blanket, Kettle and Hoover. Featured by the BBC, Wales Tourist Board, and British Holiday Home Parks. Superior Dragon Award Holiday Homes with heated Bedroom, £2 nightly. View any time. Try a £12 minibreak.

MARCH				APRIL				MAY				JUNE				JULY				AUGUST				SEPTEMBER				OCTOBER			
Date	6 berth	8 berth	10 berth	Date	6 berth	8 berth	10 berth	Date	6 berth	8 berth	10 berth	Date	6 berth	8 berth	10 berth	Date	6 berth	8 berth	10 berth	Date	6 berth	8 berth	10 berth	Date	6 berth	8 berth	10 berth	Date	6 berth	8 berth	10 berth
12	£35	£38	£40	2BH	£49	£69	£79	7	£43	£55	£57	4	£69	£89	£95	2	£109	£129	£139	6	£155	£189	£199	3	£79	£99	£109	1	£39	£45	£55
19	£37	£39	£42	9	£39	£49	£52	14	£45	£57	£59	11	£79	£99	£105	9	£115	£139	£145	13	£155	£189	£199	10	£65	£79	£85	8	£35	£45	£49
26GF	£39	£55	£59	16	£39	£45	£47	21	£49	£67	£69	18	£89	£115	£119	16	£135	£169	£179	20	£155	£185	£199	17	£49	£65	£75	15	£35	£47	£49
				23	£39	£45	£47	28BH	£99	£129	£155	25	£99	£119	£129	23	£155	£189	£199	27BH	£129	£159	£169	24	£45	£55	£63	22	£45	£59	£65
				30MD	£41	£49	£53									30	£155	£189	£199												

12 foot wide super luxury holiday homes, 20% more spacious. Add £35 to above prices. Deposit £25 p.w. and Insurance £1 nightly. Sea view £2 nightly.
Twin bedded room £2 nightly. Superior Dragon Award, with heated bedroom £2 nightly, latest model, recent model, up market model, double glazed model heated to 70°, special position, upgraded etc £5 nightly each. Request quotation. Over 6 persons £3 per night each. (Dogs £2 nightly). Weekends, Midweek or Week Breaks Phone 0286 660400.

BEACH HOLIDAY, WEST POINT, THE BEACH, PONTLLYFNI, CAERNARFON, NORTH WALES LL54 5ET

PERSONAL ATTENTION, BROCHURE
& RESERVATIONS TEL 0286 660400

GUIDE TO
CARAVAN AND CAMPING HOLIDAYS 1994

Caravans for Hire,
Caravan Sites and Night Halts, Holiday Parks
and Centres, and Camping Sites

FHG

Other FHG Publications 1994

Recommended Short Break Holidays in Britain
Recommended Country Hotels of Britain
Recommended Wayside Inns of Britain
Pets Welcome!
Bed and Breakfast in Britain
The Golf Guide: Where to Play/Where to Stay
Farm Holiday Guide England, Wales, Ireland & Channel Islands
Farm Holiday Guide Scotland
Self Catering and Furnished Holidays
Britain's Best Holidays
Bed and Breakfast Stops
Children Welcome! Family Holiday Guide

Typeset by R.D. Composition Ltd., Glasgow.
Printed and bound by Benham's Ltd., Colchester.

Distribution – **Book Trade**: WLM, 117 The Hollow, Littleover, Derby DE3 7BS (Tel: 0332 272020. Fax: 0332 774287).
News Trade: UMD, Castle House, 37/45 Paul Street, London EC2A 4PB. (Tel: 071-490 2020. Fax: 071-490 1239).

Published by FHG Publications Ltd.,
Abbey Mill Business Centre, Seedhill, Paisley PA1 1TJ   (Tel: 041-887 0428. Fax: 041-889 7204).
A member of the U.N. Group.

CONTENTS

We have included the following symbols:

- Caravans for Hire (One or more caravans for hire on a site)
- Holiday Parks and Centres (Usually larger sites hiring holiday homes/vans, with amenities)
- Caravan Sites (For touring caravans, caravanettes, etc.)
- Camping Sites (Where campers are welcome).

FOREWORD

The FHG Guide to
CARAVAN & CAMPING HOLIDAYS 1994

Of all the holidays booked in Britain by the British, about a quarter are spent in caravan accommodation. Renting or staying in your own van on a site attracts most people but almost a third prefer the freedom of touring. Taken together, caravans and camping are our single most popular form of holiday accommodation – more popular than guesthouses, more popular even than staying in a hotel.

And why not! Looking at the hundreds of entries in our *GUIDE TO CARAVAN & CAMPING HOLIDAYS* for 1994, most sites have modern facilities and excellent amentities and today's caravan itself lacks few of the comforts of home.

To add hopefully to your holiday enjoyment, we have arranged with the proprietors and managers of a range of holiday attractions to offer our readers FREE or REDUCED RATE entry during 1994. If you turn over a few pages, you'll see a clearly marked selection of Voucher/Coupons which you should cut out and use as appropriate.

Our entries are classified by country and county in separate sections for Caravans for Hire, Holiday Parks and Centres, Caravan Sites and Night Halts, and for Camping Sites. We hope that we have provided all the details you will require for direct bookings with proprietors and managers and that you may also find the following suggestions helpful

ENQUIRIES AND BOOKINGS. Give full details of dates (with an alternative), numbers and any special requirements. Ask about any points in the holiday description which are not clear and make sure that prices and conditions are clearly explained. You should receive confirmation in writing and a receipt for any deposit or advance payment.

If you book your holiday well in advance, especially self-catering, confirm your arrival details nearer the time.

CANCELLATIONS. A holiday booking is a form of contract with obligations on both sides. If you have to cancel, give as much notice as possible. The longer the notice the better the chance that your host can replace your booking and therefore refund any payments. If the proprietor cancels in such a way that causes serious inconvenience, he may have obligations to you which have not been properly honoured. Take advice if necessary from such organisations as the Citizen's Advice Bureau, Consumer's Association, Trading Standards Office, Local Tourist Office, etc., or your own solicitor.

COMPLAINTS. It's best if any problems can be sorted out at the start of your holiday. You should therefore try to raise any complaints on the spot. If you do not, or if the problem is not solved, you can contact the organisations mentioned above. You can also write to us. We will follow up the complaint with the advertiser – but we cannot act as intermediaries or accept responsibility for holiday arrangements.

FHG Publications Ltd. do not inspect accommodation and an entry in our guides does not imply a recommendation. However our advertisers have signed their agreement to work for the holidaymaker's best interests and as their customer, you have the right to expect appropriate attention and service.

HOLIDAY INSURANCE. It is possible to insure against holiday cancellation. Brokers and insurance companies can advise you about this.

The FHG DIPLOMA. Every year we award a small number of diplomas to holiday proprietors whose services have been specially commended by our readers. Please let us know if you have had an outstanding holiday experience so that we can give due recognition.

For popular locations, especially during the main holiday season, you should always book in advance. Please mention the FHG *GUIDE TO CARAVAN & CAMPING HOLIDAYS* when you are making enquiries or bookings and don't forget to use our Readers' Offer Voucher/Coupons if you're near any of the attractions which are kindly participating.

Peter Clark, Publishing Director

READERS OFFER VOUCHERS 1994

FHG

READERS' OFFER 1994

VALID during 1994 Season

Beale Wildlife Gardens

Church Farm, Lower Basildon, Reading, Berkshire RG8 9NH Tel: (0734) 845172

Admit **ONE CHILD FREE** with an accompanying adult

NOT TO BE USED IN CONJUNCTION WITH ANY OTHER OFFER

FHG

READERS' OFFER 1994

VALID April to October 1994

Cambridge and County Folk Museum

2/3 Castle Street, Cambridge CB3 0AQ Telephone: (0223) 355159

Admit **ONE ADULT FREE** when accompanied by a paying adult

NOT TO BE USED IN CONJUNCTION WITH ANY OTHER OFFER

FHG

READERS' OFFER 1994

VALID during 1994

Sacrewell Farm & Country Centre

Thornhaugh, Peterborough, Cambridgeshire PE8 6HJ Telephone: (0780) 782222

One **FREE** admission with each paid entry of similar age group (adult/child)

NOT TO BE USED IN CONJUNCTION WITH ANY OTHER OFFER

FHG

READERS' OFFER 1994

VALID during 1994 Season

Flambards Village Theme Park

Helston, Cornwall TR13 0GA Telephone: (0326) 574549

£1.00 OFF full admission price

NOT TO BE USED IN CONJUNCTION WITH ANY OTHER OFFER

We hope you find these coupons useful and would welcome any comments you have regarding them

Exotic birds, pets' corner, adventure playgrounds, river cruises etc, all set in acres of gardens, lakes and water meadows.

DIRECTIONS: on A329 one mile from Pangbourne.

OPEN: daily (closed January and February).

FHG PUBLICATIONS, ABBEY MILL BUSINESS CENTRE, PAISLEY PA1 1TJ

Housed in a 17th century Inn, the Museum reflects the everyday life of Cambridge and the county from 1650 to the present day.

DIRECTIONS: near the river in the centre of Cambridge.

OPEN: daily (October to March closed Mondays).

FHG PUBLICATIONS, ABBEY MILL BUSINESS CENTRE, PAISLEY PA1 1TJ

The fascinating story of farming and country life with working watermill, gardens, collections of bygones, farm and nature trails.

DIRECTIONS: off A47, 8 miles west of Peterborough.

OPEN: daily all year.

FHG PUBLICATIONS, ABBEY MILL BUSINESS CENTRE, PAISLEY PA1 1TJ

All-weather entertainment for all the family. Victorian Village, Britain in the Blitz, rides and much more.

DIRECTIONS: A394 to Helston.

OPEN: Easter to end October.

FHG PUBLICATIONS, ABBEY MILL BUSINESS CENTRE, PAISLEY PA1 1TJ

READERS' OFFER 1994

VALID during
1994 Season

North Cornwall Museum and Gallery

The Clease, Camelford, Cornwall Telephone: (0840) 212954

One **FREE** adult entry with every paid adult entry

NOT TO BE USED IN CONJUNCTION WITH ANY OTHER OFFER

READERS' OFFER 1994

VALID Easter to end
November 1994 except
30/31 July

South Tynedale Railway

Alston, Cumbria CA9 3JB Telephone (0434) 381696

Reduction of 40p on adult ticket and 20p on child ticket

NOT TO BE USED IN CONJUNCTION WITH ANY OTHER OFFER

FHG

READERS' OFFER 1994

VALID during
1994

Tullie House City Museum and Art Gallery

Castle Street, Carlisle, Cumbria CA3 8TP Telephone: (0228) 34781

One person admitted **FREE** for every adult admission purchased

NOT TO BE USED IN CONJUNCTION WITH ANY OTHER OFFER

FHG

READERS' OFFER 1994

VALID Spring Bank
Holiday to October 1994

Devonshire Collection of Period Costume

43 High Street, Totnes, Devon TQ9 5NP Tel: (0803) 862423

Admit **TWO** for the price of one

NOT TO BE USED IN CONJUNCTION WITH ANY OTHER OFFER

READERS' OFFER 1994

VALID during
1994

TANK MUSEUM

Bovington, Wareham, Dorset BH20 6JG Telephone: (0929) 403463/403329

50p Restaurant Voucher to be used in Gauntlet Restaurant

NOT TO BE USED IN CONJUNCTION WITH ANY OTHER OFFER

Life in Cornwall during the past century. Workmen's tools, domestic items, collection of Cornish and Devonshire pottery.

DIRECTIONS: off A39 18 miles south of Bude.

OPEN: Easter to end September daily except Sundays.

FHG PUBLICATIONS, ABBEY MILL BUSINESS CENTRE, PAISLEY PA1 1TJ

England's highest narrow-gauge railway. Steam and diesel engines carry passengers through the scenic North Pennines.

DIRECTIONS: station is just off A686 Hexham road north of Alston town centre.

OPEN: service operates April to November (daily July and August).

FHG PUBLICATIONS, ABBEY MILL BUSINESS CENTRE, PAISLEY PA1 1TJ

The story of Carlisle's place in turbulent Border history focusing on the Romans, historic railways, and the notorious Reivers.

DIRECTIONS: follow signs for Castle and Cathedral in Carlisle.

OPEN: daily except Christmas Day.

FHG PUBLICATIONS, ABBEY MILL BUSINESS CENTRE, PAISLEY PA1 1TJ

A selection of costumes and accessories (changed each year) on show in one of the oldest and most interesting houses in the heart of Totnes.

DIRECTIONS: part of the Butterwalk which is near main town car park.

OPEN: Spring Bank Holiday to October 1st (closed Saturdays).

FHG PUBLICATIONS, ABBEY MILL BUSINESS CENTRE, PAISLEY PA1 1TJ

Armoured fighting vehicles from all over the world. Drive-a-tank simulators, video theatres, restaurant.

DIRECTIONS: follow signs to Bovington Camp, near Wareham.

OPEN: daily except for 10 days at Christmas.

FHG PUBLICATIONS, ABBEY MILL BUSINESS CENTRE, PAISLEY PA1 1TJ

FHG

READERS' OFFER 1994

VALID during 1994 Season

𝔥𝔢𝔡𝔦𝔫𝔤𝔥𝔞𝔪 𝔠𝔞𝔰𝔱𝔩𝔢

Castle Hedingham, Halstead, Essex CO9 3DJ Telephone: (0787) 60261

REDUCTION of 50p per ticket (adult and child)

NOT TO BE USED IN CONJUNCTION WITH ANY OTHER OFFER

FHG

READERS' OFFER 1994

VALID April to September 1994

Cotswold Farm Park

Guiting Power, Cheltenham, Gloucestershire GL54 5UG Tel: (0451) 850307

Admit one child **FREE** with an adult paying full entrance fee

NOT TO BE USED IN CONJUNCTION WITH ANY OTHER OFFER

FHG

READERS' OFFER 1994

VALID during 1994 season

BERKELEY CASTLE

Berkeley, Gloucestershire GL13 9BQ Telephone: (0453) 810332

Admit one **FAMILY** at group rates

NOT TO BE USED IN CONJUNCTION WITH ANY OTHER OFFER

FHG

READERS' OFFER 1994

VALID April to October 1994

Hereford Cider Museum Trust

21 Ryelands Street, Hereford HR4 0LW Telephone: (0432) 354207

Admit **TWO ADULTS** at group reduction rate

NOT TO BE USED IN CONJUNCTION WITH ANY OTHER OFFER

FHG

READERS' OFFER 1994

VALID all year

The Walter Rothschild Zoological Museum

Akeman Street, Tring, Hertfordshire HP23 6AP Telephone: (0442) 824181

One child **FREE** entry with full paying adult

NOT TO BE USED IN CONJUNCTION WITH ANY OTHER OFFER

Magnificent Norman Keep with banqueting hall and minstrels' gallery.

Beautiful grounds with woodland and lakeside walks; light refreshments.

DIRECTIONS: on B1058, one mile from A604 between Cambridge and Colchester.

Within easy reach of M25, M11 and A12.

OPEN: Easter to end October.

FHG PUBLICATIONS, ABBEY MILL BUSINESS CENTRE, PAISLEY PA1 1TJ

The home of rare breed conservation, with over 50 breeding flocks and herds.

Adventure playground, pets' corners, gift shops etc.

DIRECTIONS: M5 Junction 9, B4077 Stow-on-the-Wold road.

7 miles from Stow-on-the-Wold and Bourton-on-the-Water.

OPEN: daily March to October.

FHG PUBLICATIONS, ABBEY MILL BUSINESS CENTRE, PAISLEY PA1 1TJ

Magnificent home of the Berkeley family for over 850 years.

Full of treasures including paintings, tapestries, porcelain.

DIRECTIONS: off A38 midway between Bristol and Gloucester.

OPEN: April to October.

FHG PUBLICATIONS, ABBEY MILL BUSINESS CENTRE, PAISLEY PA1 1TJ

Cider Museum and Distillery telling the fascinating story of traditional cider making through the ages. Displays include reconstructed farm cider house and cider brandy distillery.

DIRECTIONS: off A438 towards Brecon.

OPEN: April to October daily 10am-5.30pm; November to March Mon-Sat 1-5pm.

FHG PUBLICATIONS, ABBEY MILL BUSINESS CENTRE, PAISLEY PA1 1TJ

Founded by the second Baron Rothschild; unusual museum containing a fine collection of mammals, birds, reptiles and insects in a unique Victorian setting.

DIRECTIONS: Tring is on A41 between Berkhamsted and Aylesbury.

OPEN: all year.

FHG PUBLICATIONS, ABBEY MILL BUSINESS CENTRE, PAISLEY PA1 1TJ

FHG

READERS' OFFER 1994
VALID during 1994
The White Cliffs Experience
Market Square, Dover, Kent Telephone (0304) 214566
£1 DISCOUNT per admission (up to 4 persons per voucher)
NOT TO BE USED IN CONJUNCTION WITH ANY OTHER OFFER
CODE B

FHG

READERS' OFFER 1994
VALID during 1994 Season
Kent & East Sussex Railway
Tenterden Station, Tenterden, Kent TN30 6HE Telephone: (0580) 765155
TWO FOR THE PRICE OF ONE with every full fare paying adult
NOT TO BE USED IN CONJUNCTION WITH ANY OTHER OFFER

FHG

READERS' OFFER 1994
VALID until October 1994
WIGAN PIER
Wigan, Lancashire WN3 4EU Telephone: (0942) 323666
£3.10 OFF price of family ticket
NOT TO BE USED IN CONJUNCTION WITH ANY OTHER OFFER

FHG

READERS' OFFER 1994
VALID until October 1994
FRONTIERLAND
Promenade, Morecambe, Lancashire LA4 4DG Telephone: (0524) 410024
Buy one Day Pass and get another **FREE**
NOT TO BE USED IN CONJUNCTION WITH ANY OTHER OFFER

FHG

READERS' OFFER 1994
VALID Jan–March and Sept–Oct 1994
SNIBSTON DISCOVERY PARK
Ashby Road, Coalville, Leicestershire LE6 2LN Telephone: (0530) 510851
20% DISCOUNT on adult and concessionary tickets
NOT TO BE USED IN CONJUNCTION WITH ANY OTHER OFFER

From the Romans to World War II, Dover's historic past comes alive using the latest audio-visual techniques.

DIRECTIONS: from London A2(M2) or A20(M20); within walking distance of Dover Priory BR station.

OPEN: daily except Christmas Day.

FHG PUBLICATIONS, ABBEY MILL BUSINESS CENTRE, PAISLEY PA1 1TJ

Restored by a charitable trust, historic steam engines run through scenic countryside between Tenterden and Northiam.

DIRECTIONS: on A28 between Ashford and Hastings.

OPEN: Weekends in March, April, May, October, November; daily June–September.

FHG PUBLICATIONS, ABBEY MILL BUSINESS CENTRE, PAISLEY PA1 1TJ

Heritage with a difference – part theatre, part museum. The home of the world's largest working steam engine. Find out "The Way We Were" in 1900.

DIRECTIONS: leave M6 at Junction 26, M61 at Junction 6.

OPEN: throughout the year except Christmas and Boxing Days. Closed Fridays.

FHG PUBLICATIONS, ABBEY MILL BUSINESS CENTRE, PAISLEY PA1 1TJ

Western theme park with rides and attractions for all the family.

DIRECTIONS: on coast 8 miles south of M6 Junction 35.

OPEN: daily.

FHG PUBLICATIONS, ABBEY MILL BUSINESS CENTRE, PAISLEY PA1 1TJ

Five main gallery areas tell the story of the county's rich industrial heritage. Hands-on *Science Alive!*, nature trail and picnic areas.

DIRECTIONS: 12 miles north-west of Leicester.

OPEN: daily except Christmas and Boxing Days.

FHG PUBLICATIONS, ABBEY MILL BUSINESS CENTRE, PAISLEY PA1 1TJ

Rescues and rears abandoned seal pups before returning them to the wild.
Specialised collection includes penguins, reptiles etc.

DIRECTIONS: coastal resort 19 miles north-east of Boston.

OPEN: daily except Christmas Day, Boxing Day and New Year's Day.

FHG PUBLICATIONS, ABBEY MILL BUSINESS CENTRE, PAISLEY PA1 1TJ

Family-run zoo offering an opportunity to experience the sights, sounds and smells
of wild animals including many endangered species.

DIRECTIONS: on the coast 16 miles north of Liverpool.

OPEN: daily except Christmas Day.

FHG PUBLICATIONS, ABBEY MILL BUSINESS CENTRE, PAISLEY PA1 1TJ

A fun way to understand the links between farming, food and the land.
Lots of friendly animals, activity centre.

DIRECTIONS: off the A614 at Farnsfield, 12 miles north of Nottingham.

OPEN: daily all year round.

FHG PUBLICATIONS, ABBEY MILL BUSINESS CENTRE, PAISLEY PA1 1TJ

Beautiful walled garden with nearly 900 types of herbs,
woodland walk, nursery, shop. Guide dogs only.

DIRECTIONS: 6 miles north of Hexham, next to Chesters Roman Fort.

OPEN: daily March to October/November.

FHG PUBLICATIONS, ABBEY MILL BUSINESS CENTRE, PAISLEY PA1 1TJ

The golden age of the Great Western Railway – steam trains, original equipment; picnic
area and refreshment room. Rides on trains all Sundays June to August,
Bank Holidays – enquire for other times.

DIRECTIONS: 10 miles south of Oxford, signposted from M4 (Junction 13) and A34.

OPEN: weekends all year; daily April to September.

FHG PUBLICATIONS, ABBEY MILL BUSINESS CENTRE, PAISLEY PA1 1TJ

FHG **READERS' OFFER 1994** VALID April to end October 1994

Cogges Manor Farm Museum

Church Lane, Witney, Oxfordshire OX8 6LA Tel: (0993) 772602

FREE pot of tea on production of voucher

NOT TO BE USED IN CONJUNCTION WITH ANY OTHER OFFER

FHG **READERS' OFFER 1994** VALID during 1994

RODE BIRD GARDENS

Rode, Near Bath, Somerset BA3 6QW Telephone: (0373) 830326

One child **FREE** with each full paying adult

NOT TO BE USED IN CONJUNCTION WITH ANY OTHER OFFER

FHG **READERS' OFFER 1994** VALID during 1994

PERRY'S CIDER MILLS

Dowlish Wake, Near Ilminster, Somerset Telephone: (0460) 52681

10% OFF all shop goods excluding cider and cider brandy (free entry to museum)

NOT TO BE USED IN CONJUNCTION WITH ANY OTHER OFFER

FHG **READERS' OFFER 1994** VALID all year

PLANET EARTH

Garden Paradise, Avis Road, Newhaven, East Sussex BN9 0DH Tel: (0273) 512123

Admit one **FREE** adult or child with one adult paying full entrance price

NOT TO BE USED IN CONJUNCTION WITH ANY OTHER OFFER

FHG **READERS' OFFER 1994** VALID during 1994

MetroLand

MetroCentre, Gateshead, Tyne & Wear NE11 9YZ Telephone: 091-493 2048

TWO for the price of **ONE** when paying full admission price

NOT TO BE USED IN CONJUNCTION WITH ANY OTHER OFFER

A museum of the Oxfordshire countryside, with Manor House, working farm, riverside walks etc, plus daily demonstration of cooking on the kitchen range.

DIRECTIONS: follow signs from A40, close to Witney town centre.

OPEN: 2nd April to end October. Closed Mondays except Bank Holidays,

FHG PUBLICATIONS, ABBEY MILL BUSINESS CENTRE, PAISLEY PA1 1TJ

Hundreds of brilliant exotic birds in natural surroundings. Children's play area and pets' corner. Woodland steam railway (summer, weather permitting).

DIRECTIONS: turn off the A36 10 miles south of Bath.

OPEN: all year except Christmas Day.

FHG PUBLICATIONS, ABBEY MILL BUSINESS CENTRE, PAISLEY PA1 1TJ

See how cider has been made for centuries in the traditional way.
Cider shop – try before you buy.

DIRECTIONS: approximately 2 miles from Ilminster, 3 miles from Cricket St Thomas.

OPEN: all year except Sunday afternoons.

FHG PUBLICATIONS, ABBEY MILL BUSINESS CENTRE, PAISLEY PA1 1TJ

Trace the history of the world from 4500 million years ago to the present day. Journey through time and see how plants and animals lived 200 million years ago. Other attractions include World of Dinosaurs and Miniature Railway.

DIRECTIONS: signposted "Garden Paradise" off A26 and A259.

OPEN: all year.

FHG PUBLICATIONS, ABBEY MILL BUSINESS CENTRE, PAISLEY PA1 1TJ

Europe's only indoor theme park with roller coaster, kiddies' railway, live entertainment and lots more – a great day IN.

DIRECTIONS: A1(M), south of Newcastle-upon-Tyne.

OPEN: daily all year round.

FHG PUBLICATIONS, ABBEY MILL BUSINESS CENTRE, PAISLEY PA1 1TJ

FHG
READERS' OFFER 1994
VALID during 1994 Season
Cadeby Steam & Brass Rubbing Centre
Nuneaton, Warwickshire CV13 0AS Telephone: (0455) 290462
Train ride for two, and two cream teas or similar
NOT TO BE USED IN CONJUNCTION WITH ANY OTHER OFFER

FHG
READERS' OFFER 1994
VALID until 31st October 1994
DYSON PERRINS MUSEUM
Severn Street, Worcester WR1 2NE Telephone: (0905) 23221
Admit **TWO** adults for the price of one museum entry
NOT TO BE USED IN CONJUNCTION WITH ANY OTHER OFFER

FHG
READERS' OFFER 1994
VALID during 1994
Dracula Experience
9 Marine Parade, Whitby, North Yorkshire Telephone: (0904) 658775
One **FREE** admission when one of equal value is purchased
NOT TO BE USED IN CONJUNCTION WITH ANY OTHER OFFER

FHG
READERS' OFFER 1994
VALID during 1994
FRIARGATE WAX MUSEUM
Lower Friargate, York Telephone: (0904) 658775
One **FREE** admission when one of equal value is purchased
NOT TO BE USED IN CONJUNCTION WITH ANY OTHER OFFER

FHG
READERS' OFFER 1994
VALID during 1994
Yorkshire Dales Falconry & Conservation Centre
Crows Nest, Near Giggleswick, Settle, N. Yorkshire LA2 8AS Tel: (0729) 825164
Admit one adult **FREE** with each paying adult
NOT TO BE USED IN CONJUNCTION WITH ANY OTHER OFFER

Working narrow gauge steam railway, railway museum
and over 70 replica brasses to rub.

DIRECTIONS: on the A447 six miles north of Hinckley.

OPEN: second Saturday each month.

FHG PUBLICATIONS, ABBEY MILL BUSINESS CENTRE, PAISLEY PA1 1TJ

World's largest collection of Worcester Porcelain,
including magnificent Chicago Exhibition Vase.

DIRECTIONS: M5 Junction 7 to city centre, then left at 3rd set of traffic lights.

OPEN: daily except Sundays.

FHG PUBLICATIONS, ABBEY MILL BUSINESS CENTRE, PAISLEY PA1 1TJ

Dracula returns to Whitby in this ultimate horror story – special sound and
lighting effects to set the hairs on your neck tingling.

DIRECTIONS: near harbour in Whitby centre.

OPEN: April to October.

FHG PUBLICATIONS, ABBEY MILL BUSINESS CENTRE, PAISLEY PA1 1TJ

"Elsie Wagstaff's War" – just one of the exciting educational journeys through time
with lots of other extra surprises

DIRECTIONS: off Clifford Street in central York.

OPEN: daily from mid-January to end November.

FHG PUBLICATIONS, ABBEY MILL BUSINESS CENTRE, PAISLEY PA1 1TJ

Birds of prey from all round the world in re-created natural habitats.
Free-flying demonstrations daily.

DIRECTIONS: A65 by-pass from Settle to Kendal; 2nd left after Giggleswick station.

OPEN: daily except Christmas Day.

FHG PUBLICATIONS, ABBEY MILL BUSINESS CENTRE, PAISLEY PA1 1TJ

FHG
READERS' OFFER 1994
VALID until
March 1995

North East Falconry Visitor Centre

Broadland, Cairnie, Huntly, Aberdeenshire AB54 4UU Telephone: (0466) 87328

50p off entry fee (March to October 1994); £10 off tuition course (October 1993 to March 1995)

NOT TO BE USED IN CONJUNCTION WITH ANY OTHER OFFER

FHG
READERS' OFFER 1994
VALID January
to March 1994

SATROSPHERE

19 Justice Mill Lane, Aberdeen AB1 2EQ Telephone: (0224) 213232

Admit one child **FREE** with full paying adult

NOT TO BE USED IN CONJUNCTION WITH ANY OTHER OFFER

FHG
READERS' OFFER 1994
VALID during
1994

JONAH'S JOURNEY

120 Rosemount Place, Aberdeen AB2 4YW Telephone: (0224) 647614

Admit one adult **FREE**

NOT TO BE USED IN CONJUNCTION WITH ANY OTHER OFFER

FHG
READERS' OFFER 1994
VALID April to
October 1994

Scottish Maritime Museum

Harbourside, Irvine, Ayrshire KA12 8QE Telephone: (0294) 278283

Admit **ONE CHILD FREE** with adult paying full entry price

NOT TO BE USED IN CONJUNCTION WITH ANY OTHER OFFER

FHG
READERS' OFFER 1994
VALID Easter to
23rd October 1994

KELBURN COUNTRY CENTRE

Fairlie, Ayrshire KA29 0BE Telephone: (0475) 568685

One child admitted **FREE** on family visit

NOT TO BE USED IN CONJUNCTION WITH ANY OTHER OFFER

Regular flying displays throughout the day when birds are flown free. Numerous species including Sea Eagle with 8' wingspan. Falconry tuition course available.

DIRECTIONS: follow signs off A96 Aberdeen to Inverness trunk road near Huntly.

OPEN: daily March to October.

FHG PUBLICATIONS, ABBEY MILL BUSINESS CENTRE, PAISLEY PA1 1TJ

Only interactive "hands-on" centre in Scotland. Have fun finding out about science. Cafe, shop with scientific gifts.

DIRECTIONS: west end of Aberdeen, off Holborn Junction.

OPEN: daily.

FHG PUBLICATIONS, ABBEY MILL BUSINESS CENTRE, PAISLEY PA1 1TJ

Find out about life 3000 years ago at this award-winning Community Project and Heritage Museum. Lots to see and do.

DIRECTIONS: within a mile of the city centre.

OPEN: Monday to Friday except public holidays.

FHG PUBLICATIONS, ABBEY MILL BUSINESS CENTRE, PAISLEY PA1 1TJ

Floating collection of historic vessels; special exhibition, shop, tearoom. Guided tours of engine shop and historic fleet; special events and craftsmen's demonstrations.

DIRECTIONS: 400 yards from Irvine rail station. By road follow signs to Irvine Harbourside.

OPEN: all year.

FHG PUBLICATIONS, ABBEY MILL BUSINESS CENTRE, PAISLEY PA1 1TJ

Historic home of the Earls of Glasgow. Romantic glen with waterfalls, gardens etc. Adventure playgrounds, pets' corner, craft shops etc. "Discovery Wood" new for 1994.

DIRECTIONS: on A78 between Largs and Fairlie. Signposted on A760 and A78.

OPEN: daily.

FHG PUBLICATIONS, ABBEY MILL BUSINESS CENTRE, PAISLEY PA1 1TJ

FHG
READERS' OFFER 1994
VALID during 1994
Edinburgh Crystal Visitor Centre
Eastfield, Penicuik, Midlothian EH26 8HB Telephone: (0968) 675128
TWO adult entry tickets to factory tour for the price of one
NOT TO BE USED IN CONJUNCTION WITH ANY OTHER OFFER

FHG
READERS' OFFER 1994
VALID during 1994
Myreton Motor Museum
Aberlady, East Lothian EH32 0PZ Telephone: (0875) 870288
One child under 16 **FREE** with full paying adult
NOT TO BE USED IN CONJUNCTION WITH ANY OTHER OFFER

FHG
READERS' OFFER 1994
VALID during 1994 season
Crail Museum & Heritage Centre
62-64 Marketgate, Crail, Fife KY10 3TL Telephone: (0333) 450869
FREE entry
NOT TO BE USED IN CONJUNCTION WITH ANY OTHER OFFER

FHG
READERS' OFFER 1994
VALID during 1994 Season
BLOWPLAIN OPEN FARM
Balmaclellan, Kirkcudbrightshire Telephone: (064-42) 206
One **FREE** entry with each paid entry
NOT TO BE USED IN CONJUNCTION WITH ANY OTHER OFFER

FHG
READERS' OFFER 1994
VALID during 1994
New Lanark Visitor Centre
Lanark, Lanarkshire ML11 9DB Telephone: (0555) 661345
One **FREE** child entry with each full paying adult
NOT TO BE USED IN CONJUNCTION WITH ANY OTHER OFFER

Guided tour showing glassblowing, cutting and engraving; world's largest collection of Edinburgh Crystal; historic crystal exhibition. Factory shop, coffee shop.

DIRECTIONS: 10 miles south of Edinburgh on A701 Peebles road.

OPEN: daily; tours Monday to Friday, plus weekends May to September.

FHG PUBLICATIONS, ABBEY MILL BUSINESS CENTRE, PAISLEY PA1 1TJ

Motorcars from 1896, motorcycles from 1902, WWII British Military Vehicles; period advertising and motoring ephemera.

DIRECTIONS: near Aberlady between A198 and B1377.

OPEN: daily.

FHG PUBLICATIONS, ABBEY MILL BUSINESS CENTRE, PAISLEY PA1 1TJ

Small museum in 18th century house illustrating the history of this Royal Burgh and fishing village, with its picturesque harbour.

DIRECTIONS: A918 from St. Andrews, A917 from Leven.

OPEN: Easter week; 1st June – mid September; weekends in April, May and rest of September.

FHG PUBLICATIONS, ABBEY MILL BUSINESS CENTRE, PAISLEY PA1 1TJ

Award-winning open farm with cattle, sheep, poultry; pets' corner and lambs. Conducted tours daily except Saturday.

DIRECTIONS: 2 miles from Balmaclellan off A712 between Dumfries and New Galloway.

OPEN: daily except Saturday until end October.

FHG PUBLICATIONS, ABBEY MILL BUSINESS CENTRE, PAISLEY PA1 1TJ

Award-winning 200-year-old conservation village with Disney-style "dark" ride, exhibition, gift and coffee shop. Play area and riverside walks.

DIRECTIONS: off A73 south-east of Glasgow.

OPEN: daily all year round (except 25/26 December and 1/2 January).

FHG PUBLICATIONS, ABBEY MILL BUSINESS CENTRE, PAISLEY PA1 1TJ

FHG

READERS' OFFER 1994
VALID: Phone for details

Museum of Childhood

1 Castle Street, Beaumaris, Anglesey LL58 8AP Telephone: (0248) 712498

Admit one child or Senior Citizen **FREE** when accompanied by 2 paying adults

NOT TO BE USED IN CONJUNCTION WITH ANY OTHER OFFER

FHG

READERS' OFFER 1994
VALID during 1994 Season

Canal Exhibition Centre

The Wharf, Llangollen, Clwyd Telephone: (0978) 860702

FREE entry for two persons to Exhibition Centre

NOT TO BE USED IN CONJUNCTION WITH ANY OTHER OFFER

FHG

READERS' OFFER 1994
VALID during 1994 except Bank Holidays

Manor House Wildlife & Leisure Park

St Florence, Tenby, Dyfed SA70 8RJ Telephone: (0646) 651201

One child **FREE** when accompanied by two paying adults

NOT TO BE USED IN CONJUNCTION WITH ANY OTHER OFFER

FHG

READERS' OFFER 1994
VALID during 1994

RHONDDA HERITAGE PARK

Lewis Merthyr, Coed Cae Road, Trehafod, Mid-Glamorgan CF37 7NP Tel: (0443) 682036

Admit one child **FREE** with each full paying adult

NOT TO BE USED IN CONJUNCTION WITH ANY OTHER OFFER

FHG

READERS' OFFER 1994
VALID during 1994

SYGUN COPPER MINE

Beddgelert, Gwynedd LL55 4NE Tel: (076-686) 595

10% OFF full adult and child admission prices

NOT TO BE USED IN CONJUNCTION WITH ANY OTHER OFFER

Superb collection of over 2000 items illustrating the habits and interests of children and families over the past 150 years. Shop.

DIRECTIONS: 4 miles from Britannia Bridge, opposite Beaumaris Castle.

OPEN: Easter to Christmas.

FHG PUBLICATIONS, ABBEY MILL BUSINESS CENTRE, PAISLEY PA1 1TJ

Intricate models and audio-visual exhibits explain how canals were built and used. Enjoy a horse-drawn boat trip or take a narrowboat across the aqueduct.

DIRECTIONS: A5 to Llangollen.

OPEN: open daily Easter to end October (limited opening March and October).

FHG PUBLICATIONS, ABBEY MILL BUSINESS CENTRE, PAISLEY PA1 1TJ

---

35 acres of landscaped grounds and gardens with animals, birds, reptiles and fish. Children's play area, cafeteria etc.

DIRECTIONS: off B4318 between Tenby and Carew.

OPEN: open daily Easter to end September.

FHG PUBLICATIONS, ABBEY MILL BUSINESS CENTRE, PAISLEY PA1 1TJ

Journey back in time with the audio-visual presentation "Black Gold" and experience the unique character and culture of the Rhondda. Children's play area.

DIRECTIONS: two miles west of Pontypridd.

OPEN: all year.

FHG PUBLICATIONS, ABBEY MILL BUSINESS CENTRE, PAISLEY PA1 1TJ

Set in the heart of Snowdonia, award-winning underground audio-visual tours. Magnificent stalactite and stalagmite formations.

DIRECTIONS: one mile from Beddgelert on A498 towards Capel Curig.

OPEN: all year.

FHG PUBLICATIONS, ABBEY MILL BUSINESS CENTRE, PAISLEY PA1 1TJ

ENGLAND

LONDON

CAMPING SITES

PUBLISHER'S NOTE

While every effort is made to ensure accuracy, we regret that FHG Publications cannot accept responsibility for errors, omissions or misrepresentation in our entries or any consequences thereof. Prices in particular should be checked because we go to press early. We will follow up complaints but cannot act as arbiters or agents for either party.

BERKSHIRE

CARAVANS FOR HIRE

MAIDENHEAD. 🚐 ⛴ ⚕ **Hurley Caravan and Camping Park, Estate Office, Hurley Farm, Hurley, Near Maidenhead SL6 5NE (0628 823501).** √ √ √ Our family-run park is situated off the A4130 (formerly A423) midway between Maidenhead and Henley on the north bank of the River Thames. We have over one mile of riverside meadows with fishing and slipway facilities. We cater for tourers, tents, mobile campers and also have six modern caravan holiday homes for hire. The Park has all mains facilities including showers, electric hook-ups and shop. An ideal touring centre for Oxford, Windsor, London and the Thames Valley. For walkers an extensive footpath network extends along the Thames into nearby Ashley Hill Forest. We look forward to welcoming you to Hurley in the near future.

CARAVAN SITES AND NIGHT HALTS

MAIDENHEAD. 🚐 ⛴ ⚕ **Hurley Caravan and Camping Park, Estate Office, Hurley Farm, Hurley, Near Maidenhead SL6 5NE (0628 823501).** √ √ √ Our family-run park is situated off the A4130 (formerly A423) midway between Maidenhead and Henley on the north bank of the River Thames. We have over one mile of riverside meadows with fishing and slipway facilities. We cater for tourers, tents, mobile campers and also have six modern caravan holiday homes for hire. The Park has all mains facilities including showers, electric hook-ups and shop. An ideal touring centre for Oxford, Windsor, London and the Thames Valley. For walkers an extensive footpath network extends along the Thames into nearby Ashley Hill Forest. We look forward to welcoming you to Hurley in the near future.

CAMBRIDGESHIRE

CARAVAN SITES AND NIGHT HALTS

CAMBRIDGE near. ⛴ ⚕ **Mrs C. Jackson, Appleacre Park, Fowlmere, Royston, Herts SG8 7RU (0763 208229/208354).** Pleasant touring site for 15 vans, 9 miles south west of Cambridge, three miles from Duxford Air Museum. Terms £5.00 per night. Directions from Cambridge — turn off A10 at "Old English Gentlemen" pub to B1368. Site on left, through village; from Royston — turn left off A505 to B1368. Site on right, after Fowlmere sign.

FENSTANTON. ⛴ ⚕ **Crystal Lakes Caravan Park, Low Road, Fenstanton PE18 9VV (0480 498388 or 0480 497728).** Opened in May 1992. The Park is very picturesque and is only half a mile from the A604, just outside the village of Fenstanton. Excellent fishing lakes. Numerous electricity points and water points around the site; first-class showers, toilets, washing up sinks, washing machine and dryer. Free use of deep freeze, battery charging, chemical disposal point and refuse points. Children's play area, small shop and gas supplies. Open April to October inclusive. Children and pets welcome. From £8.50 to £10 for caravans, from £3 to £8.50 tents. Weekly rates available. Leave A604 at Fenstanton and follow road signs to Park.

CHESHIRE

CARAVAN SITES AND NIGHT HALTS

HOLMES CHAPEL. 🗊 **Ms Bates, Mount Pleasant Caravan Park, 60 Main Road, Goostrey, Holmes Chapel CW4 8JS (0477 532263).** √ √ √ √ Four miles north east of M6, Junction 18. Established over 35 years ago, our touring caravan paddock of one-and-a-half acres is licensed for 30 caravans and is open throughout the year. All the usual amenities are provided including electric hook-ups (prior booking advised). Toilet block with showers (charge). A basic laundry room is available. Local shops half-a-mile. Limited wintertime hardstanding available by prior arrangement. Children welcome. The Park is about one hour's drive from Blackpool, the North Wales coast and the Peak District. Goostrey has better than average amenities with churches, two good public houses, Post Office and shops. BR run a fast electric service from Goostrey station.

NANTWICH. 🗊 **Brookfield Caravan Park, Nantwich.** Situated on a public park close to the River Weaver. Facilities include shower/toilet block and children's play area. The site is open from Good Friday through to the end of September annually. No advance bookings will be taken — attendant calls daily to distribute keys and collect site fees between hours of 7 am to 9 am and 5 pm to 6 pm. Dogs are welcome. Electricity hook-ups now available. Please ring **CN Leisure (0270 69176).**

WARRINGTON. 🗊 ⛺ **Mr J.O. Walsh, Hollybank Caravan Park, Warburton Bridge Road, Rixton, Warrington WA3 6HU (061-775 2842).** √ √ √ √ Accommodation for 65 touring caravans. Sheltered grassland, hard standings, tent area. Ideal centre for touring the North West, convenient night halt off the M6, M62 and M56. Directions: two miles east of Junction 21 M6 on A57 (Irlam). Turn right at lights into Warburton Bridge Road. Facilities include: toilets, showers, hot and cold water, electric hook-ups, shops, laundry room, games room, play area, telephone kiosk, car park, Calor gas, Gaz. Open all year. AA 3 Pennants; RAC. Terms from £8 per night. SAE for brochure.

CLEVELAND

CARAVAN SITES AND NIGHT HALTS

HARTLEPOOL. 🗊 **Joy and Tony Pinto, Ash Vale Holiday Homes Park, Essington Road, Hartlepool TS24 9RF (Hartlepool [0429] 862111).** √ √ Quiet and pretty country park. Situated only one mile from Crimdon's long and sandy beach, three miles from centre of Hartlepool. Durham 15 miles, Newcastle 20. A walkers' paradise. The Cleveland Way, North Yorkshire Moors, the North Pennines, the Northumberland Coast, Hadrian's Wall and the Border Countries. Beautiful 'Catherine Cookson' country. Holiday homes for sale and hire, modern six-berth caravans and tourers with hook-ups. On site shop, laundry, showers with hot water. Children and pets welcome. Terms from £5. Open Easter to end October. Golf, stables, fishing, bowling and recreation centre nearby.

A GUIDE TO RECOGNISED CARAVAN HOLIDAY GRADING SYMBOLS

From *Approved* (√ or √ √) through *Good* and *Very Good* to *Excellent* (√ √ √ √ √), these are the symbols of the BRITISH HOLIDAY PARKS GRADING SCHEME. Operated throughout Britain by the British Holiday and Home Parks Association, the National Caravan Council and the English, Scottish and Wales Tourist Boards, the scheme covers the quality, standards and cleanliness of the park and its facilities.

In Wales, the DRAGON AWARD caravans are inspected annually to ensure that they meet exacting criteria of accommodation and amenity. A Dragon Award guarantees high levels of comfort and convenience.

CORNWALL

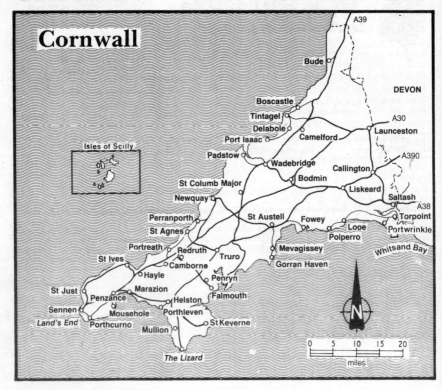

CARAVANS FOR HIRE

BODMIN. 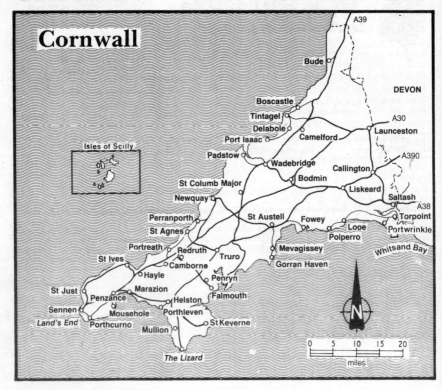 **Mrs M. J. Matthews, Pengelly Farm, Blisland, Bodmin PL30 4HR (Cardinham [020-882] 261).** A six-berth caravan situated four miles north of Bodmin on a 180 acre mixed farm, quiet and secluded with extensive views of beautiful countryside. It is central for both north and south coasts, with pony trekking nearby. Brown trout fishing also nearby. There are two bedrooms, kitchen and lounge, also toilet, shower, electricity, fridge and fire. Parking alongside van. Children are welcome and pets allowed. The picturesque village of Blisland has a shop and post office. At Bodmin there is a heated swimming pool, tennis courts, launderette and supermarkets. Weekly terms from £85.

BUDE. 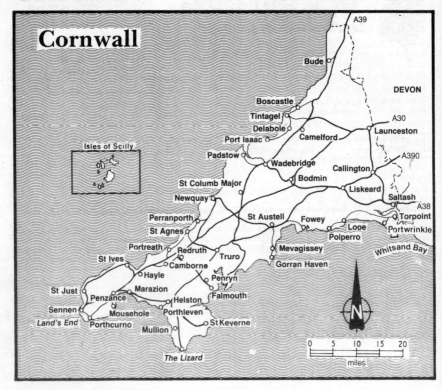 **Mrs E. Haworth, Newlands Farm, Youlstone, Morwenstowe, Bude EX23 9PT (Morwenstowe [028883] 474).** CARAVAN AND TENTS. One modern six-berth caravan. Two separate bedrooms; one bunk, one double. WC in van, shower and WC available 40 yards away adjoining farmhouse. Fridge, cooker, hot and cold water, gas fire, continental quilts and pillows, no linen. Electric light, 3-point plug sockets, television. Disabled welcome; also well behaved pets. Three touring van or tent spaces. Sited in enclosed south-facing area, picnic table and barbecue. The site offers a quiet farm holiday with coastal walks and beaches nearby. The farm is a 220-acre dairy farm on North Devon/Cornwall border, one mile from A39. Rates £50 to £130. Write or phone for details.

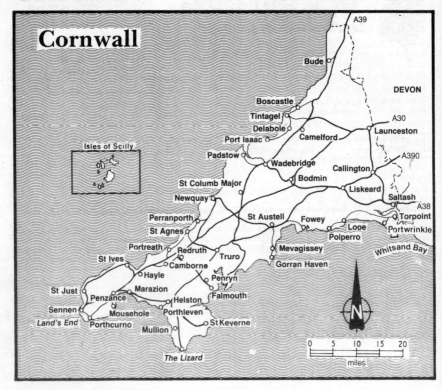 Caravans for Hire (one or more caravans for hire on a site)

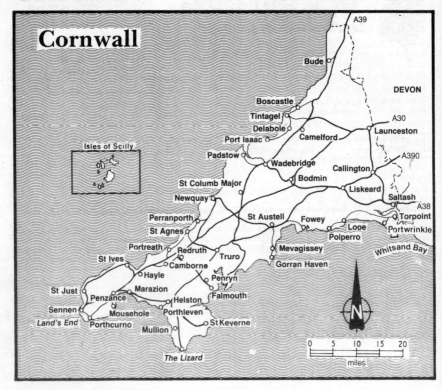 Holiday Parks & Centres (usually larger sites hiring holiday homes/vans, with amenities)

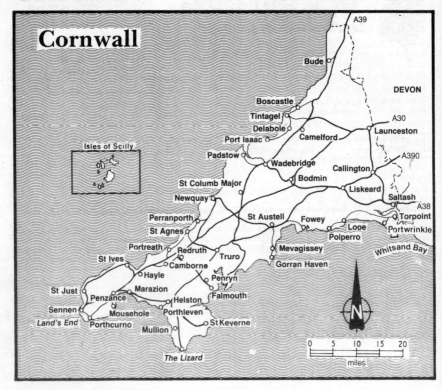 Caravan Sites (for touring caravans, caravanettes, etc.)

 Camping Sites (where campers are welcome)

WOODA FARM
CARAVAN & CAMPING PARK
LUXURY HOLIDAY HOMES
FIRST CLASS FACILITIES FOR CAMPERS & TOURERS
Caravan Club Approved   Camping Club of Great Britain   West Country Tourist Board Rec.

AMIDST SOME OF THE FINEST COASTAL SCENERY & SANDY BEACHES ON DEVON & CORNWALL'S BORDERS
A real Cornish welcome from Mr & Mrs Colwill and Family to:

EXCELLENT

Enjoy a farm and seaside holiday with us. Set in 12 acres of parkland with woodland walks, own coarse fishing, exciting play area for the children. Shop, laundrette, modern toilet shower blocks. Peace and quiet. Local village inn just a few minutes walk. Fun golf course. Licensed farm restaurant. Excellent beaches nearby. A superb touring centre for many attractions. Glorious views over surrounding countryside and Bude Bay. Indoor archery, pony trekking and friendly farm animals. Colour brochure.

AA ▶▶▶   Mrs F.G. Colwill, Wooda Farm Caravan & Camping Park, Poughill, Bude, Cornwall
Telephone: (0288) 352069   Fax: (0288) 355258

CALLINGTON. Trehorner Farm Holiday Park, Lower Metherell, Callington PL17 8BJ (0579 51122). √ √ √ √ √ Nestling in the quaint village of Lower Metherell in the beautiful Tamar Valley, Trehorner Farm Holiday Park offers peace and tranquillity. Our 15 Rose Award caravan holiday homes are equipped to the highest standard. A well stocked shop, health and fitness barn, sauna and solarium are available along with a charmingly secluded heated outdoor swimming pool. Plymouth and Looe are just half an hour away and many other tourist attractions are within easy reach. The 15th century village inn provides good home cooking. The park offers a chance to relax and unwind. Why not come and meet our friendly animals.

HELSTON. Boscrege Caravan Park, Ashton, Helston TR13 9TG (0736 762231). √ √ √ √ √ 26 luxury caravans situated in beautiful landscaped gardens in a sheltered and level park. Our caravans have two bedrooms, shower, toilet, fridge, colour TV and heating. They are meticulously cleaned and attention is given to the smallest details. We have touring and camping pitches with hook-ups and excellent new shower and toilet facilities with FREE hot water. Laundry room and shop on site. No club or bar but peaceful holidays with the personal touch. Ideal position for touring with Penzance, Land's End, Falmouth, St. Ives, Porthleven and The Lizard within a 20-mile radius.

LIZARD. Tom and Linda Gibson, Gwendreath Farm Caravan Park, Kennack Sands, Ruan Minor, Helston TR12 7LZ (0326 290666). We are a small, quiet, tree-lined family park overlooking the sea with thirty holiday caravans and plenty of space for tents and tourers. Our reasonably priced caravans all have water, free gas and electricity, and two bedrooms. Most have showers and toilets. Two clean, safe, sandy beaches are a short woodland walk away and the local village of Kuggar with pub restaurant, craft centre, pottery, gift shop etc., is within a five minute walk. The park is surrounded by miles of unspoilt coastline with cliff walks and sandy coves preserved by the National Trust as an area of Outstanding Natural Beauty.

MITHIAN, near St. Agnes. Mrs Jenny Osborne, Mellowvean, Mithian, St. Agnes TR5 0QA (0872 553274). Sleeps 4. This single caravan/chalet is situated in a peaceful spot with its own lawn and garden on a two and a half acre smallholding. Mithian's central location makes it an ideal base for touring the whole of Cornwall. St. Agnes village offers good shops, pub, restaurants, beach etc. The accommodation comprises a caravan which has been extended to include a separate bedroom, flush toilet with handbasin, and a large porch. All-electric facilities include a cooker, fridge, water heater and colour TV. A shower is available and there is ample parking. Terms from £55 to £135 per week including electricity.

FREE and REDUCED RATE Holiday Visits!
Don't miss our Reader's Offer Vouchers
on pages 13 to 31.

PADSTOW. 🏕 💲 🏕 **Mrs M.J. Raymont, Trevean Farm, St. Merryn, Padstow PL28 8PR**

(Padstow [0841] 520772). Small, pleasant site close to several sandy beaches, with good surfing and lovely, golden sands. Rural area with splendid sea views. Riding school and golf club within two miles. Village shops one mile. Sea and river fishing nearby. Padstow four miles. Camel Estuary four miles. Three static king-size six-berth caravans with cooker, fridge, mains water, electric lights — fully equipped except linen. Site provides water supply, flush toilets, showers; milk supplied from farm. Good approach from B road. Children welcome, pets permitted (dogs must be kept on lead). Weekly rates for static vans from £100 to £200 according to season; from £4 per night for touring caravans and tents. Tourers and campers welcome. Open Easter to October.

PAR. 🏕 **Mr and Mrs S.J. Guiver, The Ship Inn, Polmear, Par PL24 2AR (Par [0726] 812540).** The

caravans are situated in a private park, immediately behind the 200-year-old Inn, with a large lawn in the centre. There is ample parking space beside each van. All have mains services including full size cookers, fridges, flush toilets, showers and hot and cold water. Colour TV is also included in the price. Everything is provided except linen. Two minutes from lovely sandy beach, completely safe for children. The Inn is noted for its inexpensive snacks, including steaks and fresh fish, and there is a very pleasant garden for the children to play in whiie parents enjoy a refreshment. Cornish bands play in the garden every Wednesday and Sunday during the season. There is a family room, laundry room and bars including garden bar. Children very welcome. No pets, please. Terms on application.

PENZANCE. 🏕 **C. Hichens, Carne Cottage, Morvah, Pendeen, Penzance TR19 7TT (Penzance**

[0736] 788309). Carne Farm is situated on the North Cornish coast one mile from the nearest beach at Portherras Cove. It is an excellent walking area with breathtaking views of fields, moorlands and sea, yet visitors are only six miles from the lovely town of Penzance and two miles from the nearest village shops, pubs and restaurant at Pendeen. The spacious six/eight berth caravan with double bedroom, bunkroom, shower and toilet is located in the field beside the beautiful farmhouse. It is fully supplied with electricity, fridge, full-size electric cooker, electric fire, duvets, utensils and hot and cold water. Car parking nearby. Linen not provided. Visitors welcome on the farm. Pets by arrangement. Babysitter usually available. Rates from £80 to £130 plus electricity. Available all year round. Please ring or send SAE.

PERRANPORTH (Newquay Coast). 🏕 **Blue Seas Holidays, Perranporth.** Cornwall Tourist Board

Blue Seas Holiday Caravans

in Perranporth - Cornwall

Mrs. M.R. Caple.
'Dunroamin'
Newquay Rd., Goonhavern,
Nr. Truro, Cornwall. TR4 9QD
Telephone (0872) 572176
For all enquiries.

registered. For hire, six-berth caravans with shower, fridge, colour TV; all with sea or beach views. This is a quiet family park with shop, laundry, telephone, just 10 minutes' walk on pavement to shops and Perranporth's three miles of golden sands. The park is central for touring throughout Cornwall. Perranporth boasts many amenities including golf, tennis, bowls, putting green, boating lake, riding, surfing and coarse fishing at Bolingey lakes. Weekly prices from £70 to £295 (NO VAT); free gas and electricity. Reductions for two/four persons in low season. All enquiries to: **Mrs M.R. Caple, 'Dunroamin', Newquay Road, Goonhavern, Near Truro TR4 9QD (0872 572176).**

FHG PUBLICATIONS LIMITED publish a large range of well-known accommodation guides. We will be happy to send you details or you can use the order form at the back of this book.

PORTHTOWAN.  **Tregoyne, Eastcliff, Porthtowan, Truro.** "Great Value Holidays". Tregoyne is a small owner-run caravan and chalet park offering sound, well-managed accommodation in a sheltered valley quarter of a mile from a large sandy beach which is also renowned for its good surf. The famous Cornish Coastal Path abuts onto the park and much of the surrounding coastline is designated an Area of Outstanding Natural Beauty. Choose from our modern luxury caravans or our budget holiday caravans all offering discounts on local attractions and services. Call now or send for your free information pack quoting FHG: **Trelin (Cornwall) Ltd, Tremarle Home Park, North Roskear, Camborne TR14 0AR (0209 612738).**

ST. MARTIN. Mrs J. Jenkin, Mudgeon Farm, St. Martin, Helston TR12 6BZ (0326 231202). Here, there are only two modern, fully equipped six and eight-berth caravans, in a quiet setting on a dairy farm near the Helford River and on the Lizard Peninsula. The large grassed site, with easy access by car, is ideal for children. Helford River, including Frenchman's Creek, can be reached by beautiful walks through the wooded countryside. The market town of Helston is eight miles away and has indoor swimming pool and squash courts. Facilities for boating, sailing, fishing and swimming are nearby. The six-berth has one double bedroom while the eight-berth has two bedrooms, one with double bed, the other with bunk beds. They both have kitchen/lounge with gas cooker, fridge, kettle, toaster, colour TV and heater. Bathroom with flush toilet, shower and vanity unit. Bedding provided but not linen. Available all year. Weekly terms from £75 to £170 inclusive of gas and electricity.

HOLIDAY PARKS AND CENTRES

St MABYN
SUNSHINE HOLIDAY PARK

Near Bodmin
CORNWALL

AA

TOURING CARAVANS & CAMPING
Self-contained Bungalows & Caravans

Paddling Pool • Watershute
Licensed Bar with Children's facilities

An ideal centre for your holiday, set in quiet countryside within easy reach of safe, sandy beaches for surfing and swimming. Pony trekking on the moors, golf, sailing & fishing nearby.
Luxury caravans . Spacious Holiday Bungalows . Laundry with driers, large self-service shop . Games Room . Restaurant and Bar Snacks
ST MABYN HOLIDAY PARK, LONGSTONE ROAD, ST MABYN,
Near BODMIN, CORNWALL PL30 3BY.
TELEPHONE (020 884) 236

See also Colour Display Advertisement HAYLE. 🚐 ☼ 💲 👤 **Mr O. White, St. Ives Bay Holiday Park, Upton Towans, Hayle TR27 5BH (0736-752274 — 24 Hour Service).** Chalets sleeping 2/4/5/6 persons (luxury to budget); Caravans sleeping 2/3/4/5/6/8; Camping — bookable pitches, hook-ups, all sanitary facilities. PANORAMIC VIEWS, PRIVATE ACCESS TO THREE MILES OF SANDY BEACH, SUPERMARKET.

PERRANPORTH. 🚐 ☼ **Perranporth Caravan Holidays, Gear Sands, Perranporth.** Central for touring Cornwall's 'Poldark' country and the Cornish Riviera. Some seven miles from Newquay, astride the Coastal Footpath and approximately 700 yards to the beach. The caravans all have sea views and sleep from four to eight in two or three bedrooms. Fully equipped except linen. All have toilet, shower, colour TV, fridge and full-size cooker, plus hot water systems. Pets welcome at certain times by arrangement. Restaurant, shops, live entertainment and indoor and outdoor swimming pools with waterslide. Open from Easter to October. Terms from £80 to £400 per week. On arrival visitors are supplied with details of the many nearby holiday activities. Also available, bungalow, sleeping six. Member of BHHPA. Further details from **Mr C.C. Abram, No. 1 Crow Hill, Perranporth TR6 0DG (0872 572385 24 hours).**

Newquay Holiday Parks *are great!*

AA

For families & couples young and old.

Choose from three Parks all with the highest standard facilities, excellent services and great, great value for money.

- **Newquay Tourist Park** - fun & entertainment in South facing parkland
- **Holywell Bay Holiday Park** - next to a safe, sandy beach
- **Crantock Beach Holiday Park** - with lovely sea views in a peaceful setting

Great choice ● Great locations ● Great fun!

Phone for a colour brochure now!

(0637) 871111 *Please ask for extension 15.*

EXCELLENT

ROSE AWARD 1994

Newquay Holiday Parks Ltd, 15 Newquay Tourist Park, Newquay, Cornwall TR8 4HS

PAR SANDS HOLIDAY PARK

The Park on the beach

- Next to large, safe, sandy beach
- Indoor heated swimming pool
- Lots of open grassy space
- Playground ● Tennis Courts
- Bowling Green ● Crazy Golf
- Amusements & Pool
- Cafe & Shop ● Launderette
- Attractive wildlife lake
- Adjacent to Par Village
- Pets welcome ● Perfect base for South Cornwall.

Tents & Tourers welcome
● Good shower, toilet & other facilities ● Electric hook-ups.

Choice of **new** luxury caravans for families of all sizes ● With fully fitted kitchen, lounge & separate bedrooms ● Shower, flush w.c., fridge & colour T.V.

**Colour brochure from:
Par Sands Holiday Park,**
Par Beach, St Austell Bay,
Cornwall PL24 2AS.
Tel: St. Austell (0726) 812868

ROSE AWARD CARAVAN HOLIDAY PARKS

CARAVAN SITES AND NIGHT HALTS

See also Colour Display Advertisement **BUDE.** 🔊 ⚠ **Budemeadows Touring Holiday Park, Bude EX23 0NA (0288 361646).** ✓ ✓ ✓ ✓ ✓ AA Four Pennants; RAC Listed. With 100 pitches in nine and a half acres of landscaped grounds, you can be sure there is NO OVERCROWDING! Ideally situated just one mile from the renowned surfing beach of Widemouth Bay. We offer heated outdoor pool and separate heated toddlers' pool; TV lounge and games room; giant chess; barbecues; logland playground. We provide award-winning loos, dishwashing facility, shop, laundry. We charge per person — from £3.50 per adult per night — no additional charges for what you bring. Discounts for early bookings. Children and pets welcome. No charge for hot water, showers, hairdryers, swimming pool. The spectacular coastal scenery within easy reach is also free. The park is three miles south of Bude on A39. Please write or phone for free brochure.

Key to Tourist Board Ratings

The Crown Scheme
(England, Scotland & Wales)

Covering hotels, motels, private hotels, guesthouses, inns, bed & breakfast, farmhouses. Every Crown classified place to stay is inspected annually. *The classification:* Listed then 1-5 Crown indicates the range of facilities and services. Higher quality standards are indicated by the terms APPROVED, COMMENDED, HIGHLY COMMENDED and DELUXE.

The Key Scheme
(also operates in Scotland using a Crown symbol)

Covering self-catering in cottages, bungalows, flats, houseboats, houses, chalets, etc. Every Key classified holiday home is inspected annually. *The classification:* 1-5 Key indicates the range of facilities and equipment. Higher quality standards are indicated by the terms APPROVED, COMMENDED, HIGHLY COMMENDED and DELUXE.

The Q Scheme
(England, Scotland & Wales)

Covering holiday, caravan, chalet and camping parks. Every Q rated park is inspected annually for its quality standards. The more ✓ in the Q – up to 5 – the higher the standard of what is provided.

BUDE. 🚐 💲 🏕 **Cornish Coasts Caravan and Camping Park, Middle Penlean, Poundstock, Widemouth Bay, Near Bude EX23 0DR (Widemouth Bay [0288] 361380).** Our site is liked for what it hasn't got — no club, no disco, no hassle — just peace and quiet and a place to relax and enjoy the glorious views over countryside and sea. Two miles from the nearest beach and central for touring the north coast of Cornwall and Devon. Toilets, showers, laundry room. Electric hook-ups. Children's play area and a shop on site. 78 touring pitches, level and slightly sloping. Luxury six to eight berth holiday caravans to let. Tourist Board registered. Booking is advisable in peak season. Terms on request. SAE please for brochure.

LAND'S END. 💲 🏕 **Cardinney Caravan and Camping Park, Land's End TR19 6HJ (March to**

October: 0736 810880; November to February: 0323 841198). √ √ √ √ This peaceful family-run site is set in picturesque countryside. There are 105 spacious pitches, 50 with electric hook-ups, 17 hard standings. It has a well stocked shop, licensed café/takeaway, laundry room, games and TV rooms, modern toilet block and campers' cook room. Ideally situated for touring the south-west peninsula with its many sandy beaches including Sennen Cove with its Blue Flag Award. The famous Minack Open Air Theatre, numerous cliff top walks and climbs are within two/four miles of the site. Trips to the Isle of Scilly by skybus, helicopter or boat. Children and pets welcome. Terms from £4 to £5.50 per night.

LOOE. 🚐 💲 🏕 **Muriel and Dennis Woodman, Trelay Farmpark, Pelynt-by-Looe PL13 2JX (0503 220900).** √ √ √ √ In rural surroundings between Looe and Polperro, this five-acre park takes 43 tourers/tents/mobile caravans from £5 per night, plus personally owned caravan holiday homes for hire. We also have holiday caravans for sale. On a tranquil, pretty park with friendly owners who have time for a chat. All the marvellous Cornish attractions are within easy reach. Cities, countryside, fun shopping, interesting little towns and bays. Half a mile south of Pelynt on B3359 off the A387 Looe/Polperro Road. All the sports you could want around the quiet haven of Trelay. Controlled dogs welcome. Telephone for full details.

PERRANPORTH. 💲 🏕 **Rosehill Farm Tourist Park, Perranporth, Truro TR4 9LA (0872 572448).** AA Three Pennants. This seven-acre touring park offers level and sloping meadowland with distant country views and sheltering Cornish hedges. Our friendly and relaxing park is ideally located for touring Cornwall. We are only five minutes' drive from Perranporth's golden sandy beaches; take the B3285 half a mile west of Goonhavern village. On site we provide free hot showers; electric hook-ups are available, also laundry, games/TV room, children's playground, dog-walking field and shop. Concessionary fees at local golf club, and there are facilities nearby for coarse/sea fishing, horse riding, surfing, gliding and walking. Pub and takeaway just a short walk away. Discounts for advance bookings and for Senior Citizens in low season. Children and pets welcome. Terms: pitch and two adults, from £5 to £8. Brochure available from Resident Proprietors, LES & SUE ROLFE. Be assured of a warm welcome.

PLEASE ENCLOSE A STAMPED ADDRESSED ENVELOPE WITH ENQUIRIES

THE LIZARD. 🔊 Å **Henry's Campsite, The Lizard.** A small, family-run, friendly site for quiet "get-away-from-it-all" holidays. Situated at the top of Caerthillian Valley with splendid sea views and spectacular sunsets. The Coastal Footpaths run alongside, and many beaches, both popular and secluded, to choose from here on The Lizard Peninsula; there are three within twenty minutes' walk plus the famous National Trust-owned Kynance Cove a few minutes' drive away, with a shop, café, toilets and car park. Our campsite offers shower facilities, toilets and freshwater taps. Pets and children are welcome. We accept both caravans/tourers and tents, from £4.00 per night. Despite our seclusion, the village centre is just a minute's walk away, with Post Office, pub, shops, fish and chips and cafés. Bookings taken. For details write (SAE) or telephone: **Mr R.H.R. Lyne, Caerthillian Farm, The Lizard, Helston TR12 7NX (0326 290596).**

TRURO. 🔊 Å **Mr and Mrs C.R. Simpkins, Summer Valley Touring Park, Shortlanesend, Truro**

TR4 9DW (0872 77878). √ √ √ √ Situated just two miles from Truro, Cornwall's Cathedral City, and ideally placed as a centre for touring all parts of Cornwall. This quiet small, secluded site is only one and a half miles from the main A30 and its central situation is advantageous for North Cornwall's beautiful surfing beaches and rugged Atlantic coast or Falmouth's quieter and placid fishing coves. Horse riding, fishing and golf are all available within easy distance. This compact site is personally supervised by the owners. Facilities include a new toilet block with free hot water, washing cubicles, showers, shaving points, launderette, iron, hairdryer, etc; caravan electric hook-ups; children's play area. Licensed shop with dairy products, groceries, bread, confectionery, toys. Calor/Camping gas. Terms: two people, car, caravan/tent £5.50 to £7.00. SAE, please, for brochure. ETB, WCTB and Cornwall Tourist Board registered. Classification Very Good. AA Three Pennants.

TRURO near. 🔊 **Carnon Downs Caravan and Camping Park, Carnon Downs, Near Truro TR3 6JT (0872 862283).** The touring centre of Cornwall ... 10 acres of level short-cut grass and four acres of woodland. 94 electric hook-ups situated in attractively landscaped pitches — excellent toilets, free hot water to showers, personal and undercover dish-washing areas, facilities for bathing babies and young children, laundry, TV lounge. Adventure play area, free ice pack freezing and battery charging, Calor and Gaz sales. On the A39 between Truro and Falmouth. A quiet well-kept site with lots of space for everybody. Close to Creeks, King Harry Ferry and many beaches. Open Easter to October. Free colour brochure available.

CAMPING SITES

LOOE. Å **Mr Hembrow, Tregoad Camping Park, St. Martins, Looe PL13 1PB (0503 26 2718).** Situated approximately 1½ miles from Looe some 200 yards off the Plymouth/Looe road (B3253) our site has fine sea and rural views and is an excellent base for touring Cornwall. Site facilities include toilets, free showers, launderette, shop, licensed club and beer garden, exercise area for pets, etc. All under the personal supervision of the proprietor. Play area. Games room for high season. Also trout and coarse fishing on site. Within two miles of the site there are facilities for golf (18 hole course), water sports, pony trekking, fishing (including sharks!), boat trips and a number of sandy beaches. Single or block bookings are accepted with SAE or telephone.

CUMBRIA – including "The Lakes"

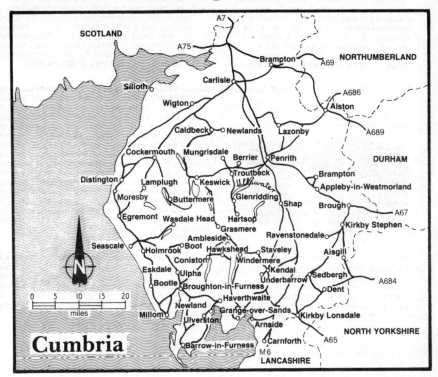

CARAVANS FOR HIRE

COCKERMOUTH near. 📷 💲 🏕 **Mr and Mrs Leslie Hops, The Beeches Caravan Park, Gilcrux, Cockermouth CA5 2QX (06973 21555).** √ √ √ √ The Beeches is a small privately owned caravan park in the village of Gilcrux, four miles from the Solway coast in the Lake District, near Cockermouth. The site provides panoramic views of the Scottish Hills. New bar and Bistro on site. Mains electricity, water and drainage are connected to all vans and an amenity block contains a ladies' bathroom as well as showers and fully equipped laundry room. Play area, overlooked by every caravan. Recreation room. Touring pitches have electric hook-ups. Caravans hired on site. SAE or telephone for brochure. Terms from £100 to £200 weekly; Short Breaks from £22 per night per van. £6.50 per night for tourers.

KENDAL. 📷 **Mrs K.M. Strickland, Grate Farm, Helsington, Kendal LA8 8AA (0539 723977).** Two eight-berth caravans set individually on a farm site in South Lakeland with open views, Kendal one mile and within easy reach of Yorkshire Dales and Lakes. Fully equipped except for linen. Vans have spacious lounge, gas fire, full gas cooker, fridge, washbasin, flush toilet and shower. Children and small pets welcome. Shops one mile. Available March to October. Terms on request. SAE please.

KENDAL. 📷 **Mrs C. Atkinson, Bank Head Farm, Kendal LA8 8HA (Kendal [0539] 721785).** One eight-berth and two six-berth caravans set on a small site on working dairy farm, with superb views. Ideal for walks, with the Lakes and Yorkshire Dales within easy reach. Shops one mile. Each caravan is fully equipped (except sheets and pillow cases), with gas cooker, electric lighting, heating, fridge, TV, etc. Complete with shower and flush toilet. Children welcome. Sorry no pets. Weekly terms from £70, including gas and electricity. Milk and eggs available. Open from April to October.

KESWICK. 📷 💲 🏕 **Scotgate Chalet, Camping and Caravan Holiday Park, Braithwaite, Keswick CA12 5TF (07687 78343).** Careful thought and years of experience have gone into the planning of Scotgate. The result is a spacious and comfortable holiday park, superbly placed between Derwentwater and Bassenthwaite Lake. All our chalets and caravans are maintained to the same high standard. We are always happy to welcome touring caravans and all types of tents. The ground has the double advantage to campers of being level and well drained. There is a shop selling groceries, newspapers and snacks. A laundry room with washing machines, tumble dryers, ironing facilities. Showers, shaver points and hair dryers are also provided in the toilet blocks. The site has its own games room with pool tables and video machines. Please telephone or write for further details.

KESWICK. 🛏 **Setmabanning Farm, Threlkeld, Near Keswick.** At Threlkeld, a genuine farm site, just

off the Keswick to Penrith road, with milking cattle and hill sheep, overlooking Saddleback with Helvellyn behind. River Glendermackin runs through the site, marvellous for walkers, within easy reach of Derwentwater, Ullswater, Grasmere and Windermere etc. Sailing, boating, steamer trips can be enjoyed. Wide choice of kingsize, excellently equipped, modern caravans with mains water and gas fires. TV. Flush toilets, hot and cold showers, shaver points, laundry room. Pony trekking. Farm and village shop. Parking beside caravans. Special rates early and late, weekends a speciality. Rates from £99 to £199 weekly. SAE to **C.M.C. Holiday Caravans, 23 Brooks Road, Wylde Green, Sutton Coldfield B72 1HP (021-354 1551).**

KESWICK near. 🛏 **Setmabanning Farm, Threlkeld, Near Keswick.** Good range of well-equipped

modern and budget caravans, four and six-berth, available on genuine farm site at Threlkeld near Keswick. Magnificent views. Convenient for northern Lakes. Site facilities include flush toilets, H/C showers, shaver points, laundry room, shop, pony trekking. Terms from £70. Early/late cheap holidays. Weekend lets available. Long SAE for details please to **Annable Holiday Caravans, 2 Spring Gardens, Watford, Herts WD2 6JJ or phone (Garston [0923] 673946) after 5 p.m. for personal response (24-hour answering service).**

LITTLE ASBY. 🛏 **Mrs L.M. Watson, Whygill Head Farm, Little Asby, Appleby-in-Westmorland CA16 6QD (07683 71531).** Two six-berth caravans on their own private site in half-acre sheltered copse near farm. Fully equipped except for bed linen. Electricity and running water in both vans. Heating and cooking by Calor gas (no extra charge). Flush toilet and hot water a few yards away, also shower and telephone. Children welcome; also pets, under control. An ideal centre for walkers and naturalists — rare plants and wildlife near at hand. Golf, fishing, swimming and pony trekking; interesting market towns, villages, craft workshops and artists' studios in surrounding area. Prices from £65 per week; weekends £9 per night.

NEWBY BRIDGE. 🛏 🔣 🛶 **Oak Head Caravan Park, Ayside, Grange-over-Sands LA11 6JA (05395 31475).** Family owned and operated. Select, quiet, clean wooded site in the picturesque fells of the Lake District. Easy access from M6 Junction 36, 14 miles A590. Static letting caravans — 6-berth, fully equipped, toilet, shower, colour TV, clean, comfortable up to date models. From £100 to £180 (+VAT). On site facilities — flush toilets, hot showers, hot and cold water, deep sinks for washing clothes, washing machine, tumble dryers and spin dryers, hair dryers, iron and deep freeze. Milk and gas on sale. Tourers (30 pitches) £7 per night (including electricity and VAT). Tents (30 pitches) £5 per night minimum. Also, bungalow for hire. Open March 31 to October 31.

PENRITH. 🛏 🔣 🛶 **J. Teasdale, Beckses Holiday Caravan Park, Penruddock, Penrith CA11 0RX (07684 83224).** Conveniently situated within six miles of the M6 motorway, this caravan park offers a choice of holiday accommodation on the fringe of the Lake District National Park. Four and six-berth caravans for hire, with mains services, electric light and fridge, gas cooker and fire, toilet, separate double and bunk bedrooms, kitchen area and lounge. Fully equipped except linen. Alternatively those with touring caravans and tents will find excellent amenities on site; toilets, showers, chemical disposal points, stand pipes, laundry facilities and shop. There is a play area with swings, etc., for children, also large recreation area. Within easy reach of outdoor heated swimming pool, pony trekking, fishing and fell walking. Some local pubs have restaurant facilities. Cumbria Tourist Board registered. Full details and terms on request.

HOLIDAY PARKS AND CENTRES

CARAVAN SITES AND NIGHT HALTS

BRAMPTON. 🛒 🏕 **Mr and Mrs T. Campbell, Irthing Vale Caravan Park, Old Church Lane, Brampton, Near Carlisle CA8 2AA (Brampton [06977] 3600).** Popular with tourists whose prime concern is cleanliness, peace and quietness with the personal attention of the owners. This four and a half acre park has pitches for 20 touring caravans, motorised caravan plus space for camping. There is a small site shop, laundry room, mains water and drainage and electric hook-ups. In fact all the amenities one would expect on a quiet, modern caravan park. We are very close to Hadrian's (Roman) Wall and convenient for having days out discovering the romantic Scottish border country. The ideal site for walking, sailing, fishing and golf. Open 1st March until 31st October. Terms from £6.50 per car/caravan plus two persons. Special reductions for hikers and cyclists. Caravan and Camping Club listed site. AA 3 Pennant.

CARLISLE. 🏕 🛒 🏕 **Orton Grange Caravan Park, Wigton Road, Carlisle CA5 6LA (0228 710252).** √ √ √ √ Small, wooded park four miles west of Carlisle on the A595, ideal touring base for North Lakes, the Borders and Hadrian's Wall. Excellent on site facilities include modern toilets and showers, launderette, children's play area, outdoor heated swimming pool, shop with off-licence, caravan and camping accessory shop. We are open all year for touring and camping and with fully equipped holiday caravans for hire on site. A warm welcome awaits you; telephone or write for brochure.

CARLISLE. 🏕 🛒 🏕 **Dalston Hall Caravan Park, Dalston Road, Carlisle CA2 7JX (Carlisle [0228] 710165).** √ √ √ √ This site on the B5299 between Carlisle and Dalston is a small well-maintained, family-run park. Set in beautiful surroundings and within easy reach of Lake District, Solway Firth and Border Counties. Open March to October it offers individual pitches, electric hook-up points, shop, hot water, showers, children's playground, laundry, games room, nine-hole golf course and fishing. Dogs are welcome but must be kept on lead. Tents from £3 per night and caravans from £6 per night. Newly developed section to accommodate luxury static caravans with all mains services. English Tourist Board and Cumbria Tourist Board registered.

CHAPEL STILE. 🛒 🏕 **Mr D. Rowand, Bayesbrown Farm, Great Langdale, Ambleside LA22 9JZ (05394 37300).** Quiet family campsite, situated at the beginning of the Great Langdale Valley. Marvellous views of the Langdale Pikes and surrounding mountains. Facilities available are ladies' and gents' toilets, complete with washbasins, and fresh drinking water from our own spring. A good base for visiting the rest of the Lake District. Several nearby pubs for good bar meals and children welcome at all of them. Adults £1.50, children 50p, car £1. Pets welcome.

GREYSTOKE. 💲 𝔸 **Mary and Colin Dent, Thanet Well Caravan Park, Greystoke, Penrith, Cumbria CA11 0XX (Skelton [07684] 84262).** Resident owners extend a warm Cumbrian welcome to our quiet, family-run park, set in lovely, unspoilt countryside, with beautiful views of the Lakeland Fells. Mains serviced caravans for sale; pitches available. We are five miles north of Greystoke, and Keswick lies 14 miles south west. Ideally placed for all the attractions and activities available in the Lake District or the Eden Valley, or as a quiet stop-over on your journey north or south on the M6 motorway. Leave at Junction 41 onto B5305 for six miles towards Wigton, turn left at signpost for Lamonby, then follow caravan signs for two miles to the park. Short and long stay tourers welcome. BH&HPA ✓ ✓ ✓ ✓ AA 3 Pennant site. Touring pitches from £6.00; stay 6 nights, 7th night free.

KESWICK. 🚐 💲 𝔸 **Mr D. Jackson, Castlerigg Hall Caravan & Camping Park, Keswick CA12 4TE (07687 72437).** ✓ ✓ ✓ Set in an elevated position in quiet countryside 1½ miles south-east of Keswick off the A591, Castlerigg is ideal for the fellwalker, with dramatic panoramic views of the mountains and lakes from the park. Touring pitches available, all with mains water, sewage facilities, electricity, all on hard standings. Modern toilets are equipped with razor points, hairdryers, hand dryers, hot showers. On-site facilities include a well stocked shop; gas exchange facility; tourist information centre; 'take away' food counter available during summer months. These amenities available all during the season. Well-behaved dogs welcome on lead. Fully serviced modern holiday caravans to let, details on request. Send SAE for our full colour brochure.

ULLSWATER. 🚐 🚽 🅰 **Ullswater Caravan, Camping and Marine Park, Watermillock, Penrith CA11 0LR (07684 86666).** Situated within the Lake District National Park, we have for hire six-berth caravans, all mains services with WC, washbasins, showers. Also self-catering holiday homes, sleep six. All mains services, TV (these available all year round). Tents and tourers welcome. Mains electric points available for tourers. Children's playground. Cafe, shop, licensed bar. Lake access and boat launching facilities. Caravan sales. Enclose stamp for colour brochure. ETB Listed.

WINDERMERE. ☼ 🟦 🅰 **Limefitt Park, Windermere LA23 1PA (05394 32300).** Come 'Up Country' and enjoy your camping and caravanning in the hills! Limefitt Park is situated in a spectacular Lakeland valley location just 10 minutes' drive from Lake Windermere. Originally a Lakeland sheep farm, the 18th century barns now accommodate first class facilities for campers and caravanners. These include The Haybarn Inn, a real Lakeland pub with country music, bar snacks and family room, the 'Campers Kitchen' where you can enjoy mouth-watering meals at down to earth prices, and an all weather Cookhouse for do-it-yourself cooking and dining. Other camp facilities include modern toilets and showers, electric hook-ups for tourers, camp shop and launderette, plus pony trekking and adventure playground. Ideally situated for touring the Lake District. From Windermere take the A592 Patterdale Road, park two-and-a-half miles on right. AA National Campsite of the Year 1992-93.

Limefitt 🏠 Park

WINDERMERE. ☼ 🟦 **Fallbarrow Park, Windermere LA23 3DL (05394 44428).** ✓ ✓ ✓ ✓ ✓ Fallbarrow Park occupies a spectacular location in wooded parkland on the shore of Lake Windermere. All 'Lake' and 'Glade' touring sites have free electric hook-ups, individual hardstandings and grass surrounds. 'Lake' sites also have individual water points. Toilet and shower facilities are first class and there is extensive foreshore with slipway and jetties. On site there is a licensed bar with good food, family lounge and children's facilities and pop bar. Mini-market with off-licence, friendly tourist information service, children's play area, launderette, etc. The park is only a five-minute walk from the Lakeland village of Bowness with its restaurants, shops, lake cruises, boat hire and recreational facilities. An English Tourist Board 'Rose Award' Park. AA Four Pennants. British Graded Holiday Parks — Excellent.

WHEN MAKING ENQUIRIES PLEASE MENTION
FARM HOLIDAY GUIDES

CAMPING SITES

CARLISLE. 🚐 💲 𝕏 **Orton Grange Caravan Park, Wigton Road, Carlisle CA5 6LA (0228**

710252). √ √ √ √ Small, wooded park four miles west of Carlisle on the A595, ideal touring base for North Lakes, the Borders and Hadrian's Wall. Excellent on site facilities include modern toilets and showers, launderette, children's play area, outdoor heated swimming pool, shop with off-licence, caravan and camping accessory shop. We are open all year for touring and camping and with fully equipped holiday caravans for hire on site. A warm welcome awaits you; telephone or write for brochure.

ESKDALE. 𝕏 **Mrs J. Hall, Fisherground Farm Campsite, Eskdale CA19 1TF (09467 23319).**

Fisherground Farm — a peace of Lakeland

√ √ √ This is camping in comfort. The spotless service centre has free hot water, showers, washing cubicles, and flush toilets. There are deep sinks for dishwashing, a laundry, and a fridge. Camp fires are allowed, pets are welcome, and there is an adventure playground for the children complete with natural pool and rafts. Eskdale has lots to offer — a miniature railway (we have our own station!); a Roman Fort, a Castle, working cornmills and hundreds of riverside and mountain walks. Several nearby pubs serve good bar meals and welcome children. Prices: adults £2, children £1. Brochures on request. **Mrs J.F. Hall, Fisherground Farm, Eskdale (09467 23319).**

WASDALE. 𝕏 **Mrs Elsie Knight, Church Stile Farm, Wasdale CA20 1ET (09467 26388).** Church Stile Camp Site is situated on a working, family farm in Nether Wasdale village. The picturesque countryside all around is ideal for fell walking, low country walks or sight-seeing in the Lake District. Facilities available on the site include flush toilets, hot and cold showers, washbasins, razor points, laundry room, chemical disposal point, mains electricity and mains water. There are plenty of wooded play areas for children. The Ravenglass and Eskdale miniature railway and Muncaster castle are seven miles away. Pets permitted. All visitors are made welcome. Tents, trailer tents and motor caravans only; no touring vans. Open March to November. Terms £5.00 per night (two persons, car and tent).

DERBYSHIRE

CARAVANS FOR HIRE

ASHBOURNE. 🚐 **Mrs H.P. Webster, "Stonehaven", Kniveton, Ashbourne DE6 1JF (0335 344721).** One large four-berth caravan situated in rural setting surrounded by lawned area, open countryside and small farms. Only two miles from market town of Ashbourne; ideal for touring picturesque Derbyshire Dales, Alton Towers, Chatsworth, Matlock Bath attractions. The caravan is maintained to the highest standard, and cleanliness and a warm welcome are assured at all times. It has two carpeted bedrooms, luxury shower room with flush toilet and handbasin, dining area, cosy lounge, colour TV. Gas fire, well equipped kitchen, mains electricity and constant hot water. Lovely country walks. Sailing and watersports nearby. Very reasonable terms. SAE or telephone for leaflet.

CARAVAN SITES AND NIGHT HALTS

ASHBOURNE. 🅂 𝐀 **Mrs L. Lane, Sandybrook Hall Holiday Park, Buxton Road, Ashbourne DE6**

2AQ (0335 342679). Sandybrook Hall is an early 19th century manor house set in delightful grounds in the heart of the Derbyshire countryside, one mile north of Ashbourne on A515. The character of the estate has been maintained by housing the amenities in original buildings — the club rooms and bar are located in a listed building and the SWIMMING POOL is situated on the site of the old kitchen garden. Sandybrook is one mile from the ancient market town of Ashbourne and is an ideal centre for touring the magnificent Peak District and Dales, visiting ALTON TOWERS, the stately homes and walking and cycling trails. AA 3 Pennant; RAC Recommended; BTA Listed; CCCGB Listed.

ASHBOURNE near. 🅂 **Mr J. Massey, Gateway Caravan Park, Osmaston, Near Ashbourne DE6 1NA (0335 344643).** When visiting Derbyshire and the Peak District with your caravan stay at Gateway Caravan Park. We are one mile from the centre of the lovely market town of Ashbourne, yet still in the heart of the quiet countryside with open farmland looking over the Weaver Hills. The facilities we offer are flat lawned pitches within easy reach of water taps, toilets and showers. Laundry and wash-up room, children's play room with colour TV. Licensed club. Chemical disposal point. Public telephone. Open from April to October. Further details on request.

BUXTON near. 🚐 🅂 𝐀 **Mr and Mrs J. Melland, The Pomeroy Caravan Park, Street House Farm, Flagg, Near Buxton SK17 9QG (Longnor [029883] 259).** √ √ √ **Working farm. Sleeps 6.** This newly developed site for 30 caravans is situated five miles from Buxton, in heart of Peak District National Park. Ideal base for touring by car or walking. Site adjoins northern end of now famous Tissington and High Peak Trail. Only nine miles from Haddon Hall and ten from Chatsworth House. Landscaped to the latest model standards for caravan sites; tourers and campers will find high standards here. New toilet block with showers, washing facilities and laundry; mains electric hook-up points. Back-packers welcome. Large rally field available. Tourist Board registered. Children welcome; dogs on lead. We now have six-berth 28ft × 10ft Holiday Van with separate end bedroom; hot and cold water; WC and shower. Fridge, full size gas cooker and fire, TV. Weekly rates only. Fully equipped except linen. Open Easter to end of October. SAE, please, for weekly and nightly rates.

BUXTON near. 🅂 𝐀 **R.J. Macara, Newhaven Caravan Park, Newhaven, Near Buxton SK17 0DT**

(Hartington [0298] 84300). Delightful site in the heart of the Peak District providing an ideal centre for touring the Derbyshire Dales, walking, climbing, potholing, etc. Convenient for visiting Chatsworth, Haddon House, Hardwick House, Alton Towers, Matlock and the Dams. Two first class toilet blocks, electric hook-ups. Children's playground, playroom, fully stocked shop supplying Calor and Camping gas, fresh groceries, etc. Laundry. Ice pack freezing facilities. Restaurant adjacent. Tents, motor vans, caravans. Pets and children welcome. Tourist Board registered, graded √ √ √ √. AA 3 Pennant site. Terms £6.25 per night. SAE for brochure.

LONGNOR, near Buxton. 🚐 🅂 𝐀 **Mr & Mrs Oldfield, Longnor Wood Over 50's Caravan Park, Longnor, Near Buxton SK17 0LD (0298 83648).** We extend a welcome to the mature visitor who will find peace and tranquillity in our quiet, well run secluded park. Ideal location for walking, and central for many attractions including Chatsworth, Haddon Hall, Blue John Mines, Bakewell, Tissington Trail and the beautiful Dales. Or forget about roads and traffic and stay on the park and enjoy a game of croquet, boules, putting or badminton, or rest and recharge the batteries. Telephone or write for brochure.

🚐 Caravans for Hire (one or more caravans for hire on a site)

☼ Holiday Parks & Centres (usually larger sites hiring holiday homes/vans, with amenities)

🅂 Caravan Sites (for touring caravans, caravanettes, etc.)

𝐀 Camping Sites (where campers are welcome)

DEVON

CARAVANS FOR HIRE

ASHBURTON. 🚐 **Mrs Rhona Parker, Higher Mead Farm, Ashburton TQ13 7LJ (Ashburton [0364] 652598).** √ √ √ √ RAC and AA 3 Pennants. Set in 270-acre working farm with sheep, pigs, cows, ducks, rabbits, geese and ponies, on edge of Dartmoor National Park. Central for touring Devon or Cornwall; Torbay 12 miles, Exeter, Plymouth 20 miles. Six-berth caravans, with all services; free heating, gas/electricity. Room for parking beside caravans. Touring site with electric hook-up (level site). Shower/toilet block, shop and laundry room. Owner lives on site and supervises cleaning — all caravans spotless. Two/three/four bedroom cottages also available. Children and pets most welcome. 10% reduction if only two occupy caravan; midweek bookings out of season. Please write or phone for free colour brochure.

BIDEFORD. 🚐 **Mrs J.A. Fox, Highstead Farm, Bucks Cross, Bideford EX39 5DX (0237 431201).**

Large and attractive modern caravan on a private farm site with fine sea views nearby. Just off the A39 Bideford/Bude road, close to the coast of North Devon and convenient for Clovelly, Bideford and Westward Ho! Luxury accommodation for six adults (sleeping up to eleven at extra charge) with bath/shower, separate toilet, fully equipped kitchen including microwave, gas fire and colour TV. Babysitting available. Pets welcome by arrangement. Linen supplied at extra charge. Shopping, beaches, local attractions and Moors within easy reach. Car essential but good walking country. Open March to October from £90 weekly low season. Reduction when only two occupants.

FREE and REDUCED RATE Holiday Visits!
Don't miss our Reader's Offer Vouchers on pages 13 to 31.

BRANSCOMBE. 🖭 🛒 Å **Mrs A.E. White, Berry Barton, Branscombe, Near Seaton EX12 3BD (Branscombe [029-780] 208).** The Caravan Park stands above the picturesque old village of Branscombe, with its thatched cottages, bakery, museum and smithy. There are two freehouses in the village, the nearest being within easy walking distance of the site. We offer a quiet, peaceful holiday for both retired people and families; there is a large area for the children to play. The site is on our 300 acre dairy and mixed farm, with one mile of coastline. We have a small herd of Shetland ponies and there are many lovely walks. Riding, golf, fishing within easy reach. Five miles Seaton and Sidmouth; three miles to the fishing village of Beer; 17 miles to Motorway. Six-berth caravans available from 15th March to 15th November. Mains water; flush toilets; mains electricity; colour TV; fridge. All caravans have toilets, showers and hot water. Laundry room; showers; shop on site. One dog per van permitted. Terms on application.

CHITTLEHAMHOLT (North Devon). 🖭 **Snapdown Farm Caravans, Chittlehamholt.** 12 only, six-

berth caravans, in two sheltered paddocks in lovely peaceful unspoilt countryside down a quiet lane on farm, sheltered by trees and well away from busy roads. Each caravan with hard standing for a car. Flush toilets, showers, colour TVs, fridges, gas cookers and fires. Outside seats and picnic tables — barbecue. Table tennis. Children's play area in small wood adjoining. Laundry room with spin dryer, tumble dryer, iron, etc. Plenty of space — field and woodland walks. No commercialism. Within easy reach of sea and moors. Well behaved pets welcome. Terms: two types, £70 to £180 and £75 to £195 including gas and electricity in caravans. Reductions for couples, early and late season. Illustrated brochure from **Mrs M. Bowen, Snapdown Cottage, Chittlehamholt, Umberleigh EX37 9PF (0769 540708).**

COLYTON. 🖭 **Mrs S.L.M. Voysey, Colcombe Abbey Farm, Colyton EX13 6EX (Colyton [0297]**

53290). Working farm, join in. Available from Easter to October, six-berth 25' spacious chalet van sited in paddock adjacent to the farmhouse on a dairy farm built on the ruins of historic Colcombe Castle. Within easy reach of several lovely beaches, and excellent shopping centre. Many local attractions include tramway, and river walks in peaceful setting. The caravan has mains electricity, fully equipped kitchen with fridge, cooker, iron, lighting. Lounge area with colour TV and heater; washroom has flush toilet and shower. Double bedroom and bunk room. Water heater and microwave. Fully equipped except linen. Ample car parking. Terms on request with SAE.

HITTISLEIGH. 🖭 **Mr & Mrs R.J. Lloyd, Whitethorn Farm, Hittisleigh, Exeter EX6 6LG (Cheriton Bishop [064-724] 273).** This five-berth caravan is very spacious, well-equipped and comfortable. Sited in a peaceful location on a working Devon farm and only three miles off the main A30 road. Convenient for the sea and Dartmoor National Park, plus a great number of tourist attractions such as the cathedral city of Exeter, 12 miles away. The caravan has mains water, utensils, fridge, mains electricity, china, pots and pans and cooker. £60 per week. Please contact **Mr and Mrs Lloyd** for details.

Terms quoted in this publication may be subject to increase if rises in costs necessitate

LYNTON. Mrs U. McCallum, Middle Ranscombe Farm, Lynton EX35 6JR (05983 258). **Sleeps 6.** One spacious six-berth caravan on a small sheep farm. Situated in a picturesque combe which catches all the sun, with wildlife to watch. There is glorious Devon countryside to explore; riding on Exmoor (stables half a mile) and seclusion and tranquillity on the farm itself. Ideal area for touring and walking, with both fishing and golf available in the locality, while surfing can be enjoyed at Lynmouth three miles away. Nearest sandy beach about 15 miles distant. The caravan is fully equipped with the exception of sheets, pillowcases and towels, and has a shower; WC. There are washbasins in the shower room and the bedroom. Gas stove, electric light and heater, refrigerator and TV. Cupboards and wardrobes. One and a half miles to Barbrook Post Office, Stores, petrol station etc. Lynton and Lynmouth are three miles from the farm. Parking beside the caravan. Sorry, no pets.

MESHAW. Mrs K. Webster, Bournebridge House, Meshaw EX36 4NL (0884 860134). This

large family caravan for four is set in a peaceful paddockside position with lovely views over woodland and meadows. Access is good and there is adequate car parking. It is a two-bedroomed Cosalt Calibre 30 model and offers the best in static caravan design. There is electricity for lighting and power, gas for cooking and hot water and mains drainage. The bathroom has a sit/bath shower and there is colour TV in the lounge. The kitchen is very well equipped. Being well off the road children can play safely within the spacious surroundings. Sandy beaches, the moors and beautiful countryside are all within easy reach which makes Bournebridge an excellent holiday and touring base. Regret no pets. Weekly rates from £70 to £140 inclusive.

SALCOMBE. Sun Park Caravan and Camping, Soar Mill Cove, Near Salcombe TQ7 3DS (0548 561378). Friendly, family-run caravan park, set amidst National Trust land with sea views and in easy walking distance of safe, sandy swimming cove. Fully equipped modern caravans with all facilities. Well equipped laundry room, children's play area and games room. Near village with good facilities. For campers we have a large, level area with some electric hook-ups and good clean facilities. Reasonable rates. Open April to October. From here you can explore South Devon and Dartmoor at your leisure. To find out more, why not phone for a brochure?

Sun Park
Caravan and Camping

SEATON. 🏕 ☼ **Axevale Caravan Park, Seaton EX12 2DF (0297 21342).** √ √ √ √ A quiet, family run park with 68 modern and luxury caravans for hire. The park overlooks the delightful River Axe Valley, and is just a ten-minute walk from the town with its wonderfully long, award-winning beach. Children will love our extensive play area, with its sand pit, paddling pool, swings and slide. Laundry facilities are provided and there is a wide selection of goods on sale in the park shop which is open every day. All of our caravans have a shower, toilet, fridge and TV with satellite channels. Also, with no clubhouse, a relaxing atmosphere is ensured. Terms from £65 per week; reductions for three or fewer persons early/late season.

Dunscombe Manor Static Caravan Park

Sidmouth   Devon   EX10 0PN   Telephone Sidmouth (0395) 513654

View over Dunscombe Coombe towards the sea.

Tucked away in a Devon Coombe is this unique Caravan Park with NO CLUB or AMUSEMENTS – just peace and tranquillity. Set in 16 acres of National Trust unspoilt countryside, adjacent to the Coastal Footpath, ideal for exploring the spectacular East · Devon Heritage Coastline and inland country walks. The delightful seaside resort of Sidmouth is 2½ miles westward and to the east lie Lyme Regis and the quaint fishing villages of Branscombe and Beer. Access to Weston Mouth Beach and is close to the renowned Donkey Sanctuary.

The fully serviced Caravans are equipped with *Toilet, Shower, Colour TV, Fire, Cooker, Fridge, Microwave, Cutlery, Crockery and Duvets*. There is a Site Shop and Laundrette. Pets by arrangement.
Holiday Caravans, New and Secondhand, sited for purchase.

TIVERTON. 🏕 **Mrs Eileen Babbage, Palfreys Barton, Cove, Tiverton EX16 7RZ (0398 331456).** √ √ √ Two six-berth caravans on 290-acre working farm, beautifully situated in paddock adjacent to the farmhouse, with marvellous views. Ideally situated for both coasts, moors and 10 miles from M5 Sampford Peverell interchange and Junction 27. Five miles from Tiverton. Enjoy a holiday in the quiet countryside with a Christian family. Lovely walks, golf, fishing and riding within easy reach. All caravans have showers, flush toilets, hot and cold water. Gas cookers, electric fires and fridges. Meter. Colour TV. Fully equipped except linen. Open March to October. No pets. SAE, please, for brochure.

WOOLACOMBE. 🏕 **North Morte Caravan Park, Woolacombe.** Well equipped modern caravans, six-berth, available on well maintained farm site. Three-and-a-half miles of glorious sand. Ten minutes' walk from site over the cliffs to Rockham Beach with its rock pools, sand and sheltered beach. Site facilities include well stocked shop, excellent toilet/shower block and laundry room. Long SAE for details please to **Annable Caravans, 2 Spring Gardens, Watford, Herts WD2 6JJ or phone (Garston [0923] 673946) after 5 p.m. for personal response (24-hour answering service).**

WOOLACOMBE. 🏕 **Twitchen House & Mortehoe Caravan Park.** Privately owned luxury caravans on popular 'Rose Award' park. Surrounded by the natural scenic beauty of National Trust land within easy reach of sea. All caravans have showers, toilets, fridge, fire, TV, gas cooking, electricity, and mains water. Our caravans are fully equipped (except for linen) to a high standard. Cleanliness is guaranteed, and every effort is made to ensure you have a carefree holiday. Site facilities. Outdoor pool, licensed bar. Entertainment. Laundry, shop, cafe. Children's play area. Sorry, no pets. Terms approximately £95 to £355 weekly. **Mrs M. Fox, 155 Headley Lane, Bristol, Avon BS13 7PP (Bristol [0272] 646822).**

PLEASE SEND A STAMPED ADDRESSED ENVELOPE WITH ENQUIRIES

FOR THE MUTUAL GUIDANCE OF GUEST AND HOST

Every year literally thousands of holidays, short-breaks and overnight stops are arranged through our guides, the vast majority without any problems at all. In a handful of cases, however, difficulties do arise about bookings, which often could have been prevented from the outset.

It is important to remember that when accommodation has been booked, both parties — guests and hosts — have entered into a form of contract. We hope that the following points will provide helpful guidance.

GUESTS: When enquiring about accommodation, be as precise as possible. Give exact dates, numbers in your party and the ages of any children. State the number and type of rooms wanted and also what catering you require — bed and breakfast, full board, etc. Make sure that the position about evening meals is clear — and about pets, reductions for children or any other special points.

Read our reviews carefully to ensure that the proprietors you are going to contact can supply what you want. Ask for a letter confirming all arrangements, if possible.

If you have to cancel, do so as soon as possible. Proprietors do have the right to retain deposits and under certain circumstances to charge for cancelled holidays if adequate notice is not given and they cannot re-let the accommodation.

HOSTS: Give details about your facilities and about any special conditions. Explain your deposit system clearly and arrangements for cancellations, charges, etc, and whether or not your terms include VAT.

If for any reason you are unable to fulfil an agreed booking without adequate notice, you may be under an obligation to arrange alternative suitable accommodation or to make some form of compensation.

While every effort is made to ensure accuracy, we regret that FHG Publications cannot accept responsibility for errors, omissions or misrepresentation in our entries or any consequences thereof. Prices in particular should be checked because we go to press early. We will follow up complaints but cannot act as arbiters or agents for either party.

HOLIDAY PARKS AND CENTRES

EXETER. Mr T.W. Aisthorpe, Springfield Holiday Park, Tedburn Road, Tedburn St. Mary, Exeter EX6 6EW (Cheriton Bishop [0647] 24242). √ √ √ √ √ One of the highest graded Parks in the area. Nine acres set in beautiful countryside. Graded level pitches with far-reaching views. 88 pitches for tourers, tents, motor vans. Luxury Toilet/Shower block with separate washing cubicles. Electric hook-ups, HEATED SWIMMING POOL, Games Room, TV Lounge, Launderette, licensed General Store, Children's Adventure Play Area. Dogs allowed. LUXURY HOLIDAY CARAVANS — six berth. Own Shower/Toilet, COLOUR TV. *FREE* Gas and Electricity. Edge of Dartmoor. Ideal touring, fishing, walking, golf (two miles). From the North take A30 signposted Okehampton, Junction 31, at end of M5 proceed eight miles and take right turn lane signposted Tedburn St. Mary. Two miles past village. Rose Award Park. AA Environmental Award. Full details and prices on request.

PAIGNTON. 🏕 💲 ⚠ **Mrs H. Burrows, Lower Yalberton Holiday Park, Long Road, Paignton TQ4 7PH (Paignton [0803] 558127).** √ √ √ √ Situated two-and-a-half miles from Paignton and five miles from Brixham. Turn off the A3022 Ring Road into Long Road at STC factory; 200 yards on right. Lovely country site of 25 acres, with all modern facilities. Modern six-berth caravans fully equipped plus touring pitches (75 hook-up sites), also tent sites available. Amenities include toilets, showers, waste disposal points and running water. Cafe, licensed bar, family room with entertainment Whitsun, July and August, TV room, heated swimming pool, amusement arcade, children's play ground, laundry room and shop on site. Open from Easter to September. AA 4 Pennants. RAC Approved. Further details, bookings and tariff on request.

TAVISTOCK. ☼ 💲 ⚠ **Mr and Mrs G. Williamson, Harford Bridge Park, Peter Tavy, Tavistock PL19 9LS (0822 810349).** √ √ √ √ √ Set within the National Park, enjoying delightful views of Dartmoor on the edge of the River Tavy. The park is flat, well drained and sheltered, with an abundance of trees and shrubs. Spacious camping for tents/tourers and motor caravans. Luxury self catering holiday homes and cedarwood chalets also available. Free hot showers, laundry room, shop, telephone; local bus service. Full range of Calor and Camping Gaz. Hard tennis court, table tennis, children's play area. TV room. Fishing (fly or spinner). Separate dog exercise field. Nearby golf, pony trekking and fun swimming pool. Please write, or telephone, for colour brochure.

TORQUAY. 🏕 ☼ 💲 **Widdicombe Farm Tourist Park, Compton, Torquay TQ3 1ST (0803 558325).** The only fully licensed Tourist Park within the boundary of Torquay. Set in an area of outstanding natural beauty with views to the sea and moors. A personally supervised (day and night) family-run site — known for hospitality and cleanliness. Excellent modern facilities. All weather sites available. Disabled suite. Baby bathroom fully equipped. Launderette, licensed bar with family area and entertainment Whitsun to September. Landscaped to provide level and spacious sites, electric hook-ups available. Very easy to find, no narrow country lanes, easy access. We also have three holiday caravans to let, all electric with shower and colour TVs. Please telephone or write for our free colour brochure. Resident Proprietors: **Mr and Mrs Glynn and Family.**

CARAVAN SITES AND NIGHT HALTS

BRIXHAM. 💲 ⚠ **Mr John Ley, Hillhead Holiday Camp, Brixham (Office: 0803 842336; Camp 0803 853204).** This family run site is situated on the coastal road between Brixham with its quaint fishing harbour, and Kingswear, which nestles beside the River Dart. The camp is set in 20 acres of camping and playing fields with panoramic views of Mansands Bay, the English Channel and the South Devon countryside. Facing south, the playing fields overlook the whole of Torbay. Facilities include FREE hot water, FREE entertainment, heated swimming pools, licensed bar, cafeteria, self-service shop, launderette and electric hook-ups for caravans and tents. Write or telephone for free colour brochure. To find Hillhead follow the A380 towards Brixham, turn right onto the A379 towards Dartmouth at Prouts Esso Garage (avoiding Brixham town centre), 50 yards after BP garage take left fork towards Kingswear Ferry — Camp 200 yards.

BRIXHAM. 💲 ⚠ **Mrs S. Love, Southdown Farm, Brixham TQ5 0AJ (Tel. & Fax: 0803 857991).** Field site with mains water. Tourers and tents welcome. Fabulous coastal views. Hot showers and flush toilets at farmhouse. Entry is signposted via Gattery Lane half-mile down Hillhead-Brixham road. Ideal situation for coastal path walkers. Handy for Brixham, Torbay and Dart Estuary. Children and well behaved pets welcome. £6 per night tourers, £5 per night tents; all-inclusive charge regardless of numbers.

HILLHEAD CAMP
Brixham, Devon

Hillhead Camp, a family-run camping site for the past 15 years, is situated on the coastal road between Brixham, with its quaint fishing harbour, and Kingswear, which nestles beside the River Dart. The camp is in 20 acres of camping and playing fields with panoramic views of Mansands Bay, the English Channel and the South Devon countryside. Facing south the playing fields overlook the whole of Torbay.

Why stay at Hillhead . . .

Hillhead Camp is in the enviable position of being close to nearly everything you could ever want from a holiday, whether it's a peaceful or energetic one. There are beaches, golf, pitch and putt, tennis, riding stables, fishing, sailing, boat trips, 5 theatres, night clubs, one of the best zoos in the country and much, much more all within 5 to 15 minutes' drive.

FREE
* Hot Showers
* Hot Water for Dishes
* Entertainment

PLUS
* Licensed Bar
* Cafeteria
* Self Service Shop
* Launderette
* Television Room
* Amusement Arcade
* Heated Swimming Pool
* Children's Pool
* Playground
* Electric Hook-ups

Facilities for Touring Caravans, Dormobiles and Tents!

Follow A380 towards Brixham. Turn right onto A379 (Dartmouth), at Prouts Garage (avoiding town centre). After BP garage take left fork onto B3205 (Kingswear Lower Ferry) – Camp 200 yards.

BOOKING OFFICE

For colour brochure telephone or write to:
**Hillhead Camp (FHG), Brixham, Devon TQ5 0HH
Telephone: Office (0803) 842336   Site: (0803) 853204**

BRIXTON. 🏕 **Brixton Caravan and Camping Park, Brixton.** Located on the A379 Plymouth to Kingsbridge road, five miles from Plymouth. Secluded and level site situated in South Devon on the edge of Dartmoor, an ideal place for touring Devon and Cornwall's beautiful countryside, moorland and beaches. Toilet and shower facilities with electric shaver points. Hot and cold water always available. Electric hook-ups. The village has a restaurant, pub, fish and chip shop, post office, butcher, greengrocer, gift shop and a local farm shop in the main street. Post to: **Mr B.H. Cane, Venn Farm, Brixton, Near Plymouth (0752 880378 day or evenings).**

EXETER. 🏕 **Mr and Mrs Paul F. Harper, Kennford International Caravan Park, Exeter EX6 7YN (Tel & Fax: 0392 833046).** √ √ √ √ √

This superb touring Park is conveniently situated just four miles south of Exeter at the end of the M5 in the heart of glorious rural Devon. With easy access to main roads and country lanes, it is an ideal centre for your touring holiday of Torbay, Dartmoor and the South West. The views from the park are beautiful, and with its individually-hedged pitches, many with mains electric hook-ups and picnic tables, it is the perfect holiday centre. Kennford International has been highly praised for its deluxe pine-panelled toilet, bath and shower complex. On the park is a large shop and gift centre with snack bar/take-away and lounge bar and our unique log fire patio is the perfect place to eat and have a drink at the end of the day. Terms: from £8 per night. Letting bungalows available. Member of "The Best of British". AA four Pennants.

EXMOUTH. 🏕 Å **St. John's Farm Caravan and Camping Site, St. John's Road, Withycombe, Exmouth EX8 5EG (Exmouth [0395] 263170).** √ √ √ St. John's Farm Caravan and Camping Site is set in pleasant six acres of pasture. There is ample room for five vans and camper vans, 30 tents; all toilet facilities including hot/cold showers. Electric hook-up points. Ample water points. Bread, milk delivered daily. Children's play area. Dogs on a lead welcome. It is one-and-a-quarter miles from shops; two miles from centre of Exmouth and Budleigh Salterton. Exeter is eight-and-a-half miles; 18 to Dartmoor. The site adjoins lovely walking country, moorlands, woods and the sea. Excellent bathing from two miles of sandy beach at Exmouth which also has bowls, tennis, golf and fishing. Many activities and many historical places to visit quite near. Terms from £4.50 per night. SAE, please, for brochure with all details. Tourist Board registered.

LYNTON. Mr Graham Giles, **Channel View Caravan Park, Manor Farm, Barbrook, Near Lynton EX35 6LD (Lynton [0598] 53349).** √ √ √ AA 3 Pennants; RAC — this quiet six-acre park, with an elevated position, on the edge of beautiful Exmoor with panoramic views over the Bristol Channel and surrounding unspoilt countryside, with excellent facilities for camping and touring caravans. Free hot showers, sinks, washing-up facilities. Launderette, irons, hairdryers, public telephone. Self-service shop. Dogs welcome on site. "Beggars Roost" Pub and Restaurant adjoining site. Luxury caravans to let with showers, fridges and colour television. Caravan sales. For details contact: **Graham and Patricia Giles.**

MODBURY. R.A. and M.D. Blackler, **Pennymoor Camping and Caravan Park, Modbury PL21 0SB (Modbury [0548] 830269 or 830542).** AA 3 Pennant Site. Immaculately maintained, well drained, peaceful rural site with panoramic views. Midway between Plymouth and Kingsbridge — A379 — it makes an ideal centre for touring. Central for moors, towns and beaches, only five miles from Bigbury-on-Sea and nine miles from Salcombe. Golf courses at Bigbury and Thurlestone and boating at Salcombe, Newton Ferrers and Kingsbridge. Large new super toilet/shower block with fully tiled walls and floors. Facilities for the disabled holidaymaker. Dishwashing room — FREE hot water. Laundry room. Play area specially equipped for children. Shop. Gas. Public telephone on site. Luxury caravans for hire, all services, fully equipped including colour TV. Ideal for touring caravans and tents. Write or phone for free colour brochure. **See also our full page colour advertisement on the Inside Back Cover of this Guide.**

SALCOMBE. ⬛ Å **Karrageen Caravan and Camping Park.** Quiet, secluded family-run site in the beautiful countryside of South Devon, overlooking Bigbury Bay. Closest site to the beaches and old fishing village of Hope Cove, one mile away. Surrounded by National Trust coastline walks and only four miles from the boating and sailing facilities at Salcombe. Modern toilet block with showers and fully equipped laundry room. Electric hook-ups available for touring caravans and tents. Bed and Breakfast also available. Please book. For brochure, contact: **Phil and Nikki Higgin, Karrageen, Bolberry, Malborough, Kingsbridge TQ7 3EN (0548 561230; Fax: 0548 560192).**

SALCOMBE near. ⬛ Å **Mr Shepherd, Alston Farm Camping and Caravan Site, Malborough, Kingsbridge TQ7 3BJ (0548 561260).** The 12 acre site, set in two camping fields in a sheltered valley amongst some of Devon's loveliest countryside one and a half miles north of Salcombe, has level accommodation for 75 touring vans with electric hook-ups available, and for 100 tents with cars. There are ample toilet blocks with hot showers, free hot water available for washbasins, and clothes and dish-washing facilities (laundry has tumble dryer), and public telephone. Camp shop sells a wide variety of goods including Calor and Camping Gaz. Pitches available for whole season for caravans up to 18ft long, also winter storage — prices on application. Information with full details and prices available on request.

CAMPING SITES

THE SALTER FAMILY WELCOMES YOU

HALDON LODGE FARM

Kennford, nr. Exeter, Devon

20 minutes from Dawlish and Teignmouth Beaches

Central for South Devon coast and Exeter. This family farm caravan/camping park set in beautiful forest scenery 15 minutes from the sea offers a family holiday and an attraction of farm animals, ponies and horse riding for novice and experienced riders exploring the forest also, 3 well-stocked fishing lakes. Weekly barbecue, country & western evening plus hay rides to a friendly country inn nearby. Many excellent facilities including – hook-ups, H/C showers, toilets, hair dryers, laundrette, adventure play area, picnic tables and farm shop with bottled gas. Set in glorious rural Devon the site offers freedom and safety for all the family. Pets welcome.

Tents from £3.50 per night; Tourers from £4.00 per night.
Personal attention given by David and Betty Salter.
For brochure telephone Exeter 832312 (STD 0392).

4½ miles south of Exeter, 1½ miles from end of M5 off A38 at Kennford services. Follow signs Haldon Lodge from Anchor Inn, turn left down through Kennford village past Post Office to Motor Bridge, 1 mile to site.

SALCOMBE near. ⬛ Å **Mr Shepherd, Alston Farm Camping and Caravan Site, Malborough, Kingsbridge TQ7 3BJ (0548 561260).** The 12 acre site, set in two camping fields in a sheltered valley amongst some of Devon's loveliest countryside one and a half miles north of Salcombe, has level accommodation for 75 touring vans with electric hook-ups available, and for 100 tents with cars. There are ample toilet blocks with hot showers, free hot water available for washbasins, and clothes and dish-washing facilities (laundry has tumble dryer), and public telephone. Camp shop sells a wide variety of goods including Calor and Camping Gaz. Pitches available for whole season for caravans up to 18ft long, also winter storage — prices on application. Information with full details and prices available on request.

WOOLACOMBE. ⬛ Å **Warcombe Farm Camping Park, Station Road, Mortehoe, Woolacombe EX34 7EJ (0271 870690).** A grassy landscaped site with panoramic sea views situated only one and a half miles from the golden sands of Woolacombe Bay. We extend a friendly welcome to our family-run park which has clean, well-maintained amenities; toilet, and shower block with permanently hot free showers; well stocked shop, takeaway food restaurant, children's play area. The perfect base for exploring the many attractions this lovely area has to offer. Children and pets welcome. Terms from £2.50 per night. Special reductions for groups in low season. To find us, turn right off B3343 to Woolacombe towards Mortehoe; site is on the right in less than a mile.

DORSET

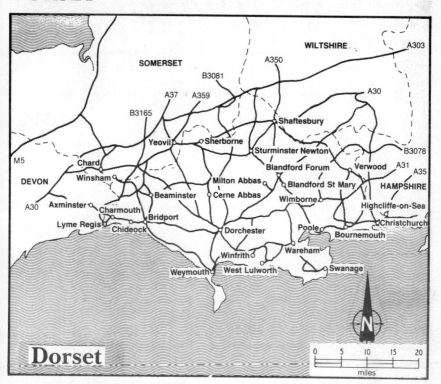

Dorset

CARAVANS FOR HIRE

BRIDPORT. 🚐 ⛺ **Mr Keith Mundy, Eype House Caravan Park, Eype, Bridport DT6 6AL (0308 24903).** ✓ ✓ ✓ ✓ A small quiet family-run park in an area of outstanding natural beauty. The Park lies on the Coastal Path and is just 200 yards from the beach, making it ideal for walkers and the less energetic. Static vans for hire from £75 to £265 per week depending on size and season. All tent pitches are terraced and have wondefful sea views. Tent charges £5 to £8 per night. Sorry, no touring vans. Children and pets welcome.

DORCHESTER near. 🚐 ⛺ **Home Farm, Puncknowle, Near Dorchester DT2 9BW (0308 897258).** Small secluded site in beautiful area, one and a half miles from West Bexington, four miles from Abbotsbury and Burton Bradstock. We can accommodate tents, touring caravans, motor caravans and also have four/six berth caravans for hire. Facilities include mains water, washbasins, showers, razor points, disposal point for chemical toilets; gas. Shop nearby. Sea fishing available locally. Good food served at the village inn. Children and pets welcome. Further information on request.

LYME REGIS. 🚐 **Mr and Mrs Corbin, Carswell Farm, Uplyme, Lyme Regis DT7 3XQ (Lyme Regis [0297] 442378).** Carswell Farm is situated in a wooded valley two-and-a-half miles from the sea. A working dairy/sheep farm with traditional jams and marmalades made on the farm. Ideal for a family holiday. Lovely walks and interesting places to visit. Two six-berth caravans with inside flush toilet and shower. Both have hot and cold water. Colour TV. Electric lights, gas fire and cooker, fridge, blankets/sleeping bags. Ample car parking. Children and pets welcome. Shopping in village, one mile. Weekly rates from £70. SAE please for terms and further details. Available May to September.

9 July £145

POOLE. 🚐 ☼ **Rockley Park Caravans, Near Bournemouth.** Please contact me for details of my privately owned caravans sited on this fabulous Rose Award Park. All caravans have shower, toilet, electricity, heating, fridge, washbasins, two or three separate bedrooms. They are fully equipped with everything you will need for your holiday. Amenities include shops, beach, water sports and fishing. Aqua Park with water slide and jacuzzi. Superb area for sightseeing. Bournemouth only seven miles. Fleet includes 1993/94 models. All caravans and bookings supervised by owner. Open March to November. From £80 to £305 per week. SAE please to **Mrs Jennifer Pretty (CC), 80 Parkway Drive, Bournemouth BH8 9JR (0202 394423).**

SHAFTESBURY. 🚐 **Mrs Talbot, Lakemead Kennels, Frog Lane, Motcombe, Shaftesbury SP7 9NY (0747 53193).** Single four/six-berth caravan with two bedrooms available all year round. Completely self-contained, set in beautiful countryside one mile from Shaftesbury. Ideally situated for walking, fishing and riding. Bournemouth, Weymouth, Bath, the New Forest and Longleat are within easy reach. There is plenty of room for children to play. Sun loungers, tables and chairs available at no extra cost. On arrival you will be greeted with a welcome pack and linen is supplied. Cleanliness is assured. From £80 to £170 depending on time of year and number of occupants.

HOLIDAY PARKS AND CENTRES

See also Colour Display Advertisement BRIDPORT near. ☼ **Freshwater Caravan Park, Burton Bradstock, Near Bridport DT6 4PT (0308 897317).** Family site with large camping fields, separate touring field and caravans for hire. Own private beach. Heated swimming pool and paddling pool. Self-service store and take-away food shop. Licensed restaurant and club complex. Hot showers; launderette; amusements. Horse/pony rides and golf courses nearby. From £6 per night inclusive for four persons. Brochure available.

DORCHESTER. 🚐 ☼ 📶 ⚊ **Mr & Mrs M. Smeaton, Sandyholme Holiday Park, Moreton Road, Owermoigne, Dorchester DT2 8HZ (0305 852677).** √ √ √ √ Quiet family-run site situated in Hardy countryside. Luxury caravans for hire, plus level grassy pitches available for tourers, motor vans and tents. Amenities include showers, washbasins, WCs, electric razor points, laundry room, Elsan point, public telephone, shop, clubhouse, games room, table tennis, children's playground and fishing. Leisure Fun Pool nearby with wave machine. Local attractions include Monkey World, Tank Museum, Sea Life Centre, and we are central for visiting Weymouth, Dorchester and Lulworth Cove. Rallies welcome.

🚐 Caravans for Hire (one or more caravans for hire on a site)

☼ Holiday Parks & Centres (usually larger sites hiring holiday homes/vans, with amenities)

📶 Caravan Sites (for touring caravans, caravanettes, etc.)

⚊ Camping Sites (where campers are welcome)

CARAVAN SITES AND NIGHT HALTS

BLANDFORD. 🗨 ⅄ "The Inside Park", Down House Estate, Blandford DT11 0HG. √ √ √ √

Situated two miles south-west of Blandford Forum on the Winterborne Stickland road, this is an ideal centre from which to explore Dorset. Offering rural seclusion, yet only minutes from the town; landscaped within established parkland on a 900-acre mixed farm with footpaths through old pleasure gardens, it offers ample space for 75 touring caravans, campers and tents etc. Within easy reach of Kingston Lacey House, New Forest, Dorchester, Cranborne Chase, Milton Abbas, Corfe Castle, and miles of varied coastline. Our facilities include WCs, showers with free hot water housed within our 18th century stable and coach house, provision for the disabled, shop, launderette, electric hook-ups, games room and children's play area, chemical disposal, gas etc. AA 3 Pennants. RAC Appointed. **Mr and Mrs W.J. Cooper, The Inside Park, Blandford DT11 0HG (0258 453719).**

BRIDPORT. 🗨 ⅄ Sue and Frank Beazer, Binghams Farm Touring Caravan Park, Melplash, Bridport DT6 3TT (0308 488234). A small friendly site opened in July 1993, set in beautiful countryside with views over Dorset's hidden valley, yet only three miles from the coast. An ideal base to explore lovely Dorset. Our facilities include a modern shop, heated toilet/shower block with separate facilities for disabled persons; laundry room and a covered dishwashing area, all serviced with free hot water. Electric hook-ups are available to all pitches. Horse riding, fishing and golf are available nearby. Pets welcome. Open all year round. Contact us for a free brochure and terms. Caravans, Dormobiles and tents all welcome.

MANOR FARM HOLIDAY CENTRE
Charmouth, Bridport, Dorset

Situated in a rural valley. Charmouth beach a level ten minutes' walk away.
Luxury 6-berth Caravans for Hire with toilet/shower, refrigerator, full cooker, colour TV, gas fire.
30-acre Tourist Park for touring caravans, dormobiles and tents.
Centre facilities include * Toilets; * Hot showers; * Fish and chip takeaway; * Licensed bar with family room; * Amusement room; * Launderette; * Shop and off-licence; * Swimming pool; * Electric hook-up points; * Calor gas and Camping Gaz; * Ice pack service; * Chemical disposal unit.
Send SAE for colour brochure to Mr R. A. Loosmore or Tel: 0297 60226

2 bed £200 . 2 bed HSE
3 bed £225 . £255 . ꒥ linen & towels

DORCHESTER. 💲 Å R. and M. Paul, **Giant's Head Caravan and Camping Park,** Old Sherborne Road, Cerne Abbas, Dorchester (Cerne Abbas [0300] 341242). ✓ ✓ ✓ ✓ This site is two miles north-east of Cerne Abbas on the Buckland/Newton road into Dorchester avoiding by-pass; at Top-o'-Town roundabout take Sherborne road, after 500 yards fork right at Loder's (BP) Garage, signposted. We are in an ideal position for a motoring, cycling or walking holiday. Places to visit include Cheddar Caves, Longleat House and Lion Reserve, Thomas Hardy's birthplace and various wildlife parks. Fishing, boating and bathing at Weymouth and Portland. Dorchester eight miles, Sherborne eleven. A quiet site with wonderful views of Dorset Downs and the Blackmoor Vale. Site facilities include toilets, water supply, showers, TV room and shop. Electric hook-ups available. Laundry room. Hot water. Children welcome, and pets accepted if kept on lead. Good approach road. Site holds 60 caravans and tents; campers and camper vans also welcome. Terms on request. Also available, self-catering accommodation.

POOLE   DORSET

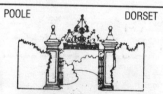

SOUTH LYTCHETT MANOR CARAVAN PARK

Camping & Touring Caravan Park
LYTCHETT MINSTER, POOLE
DORSET BH16 6JB TEL: (0202) 622577

A popular family site in rural setting just west of Poole. Ideal base for exploring Poole Harbour, Bournemouth, Wareham, Hardy country and the market towns of East Dorset.
Useful overnight stop for the Poole-Cherbourg ferry. Modern washing facilities with free hot showers.
Dogs welcome (on leads).

POOLE. 💲 Å Mrs F. Scrimgeour, **Huntick Farm,** Lytchett Matravers, Poole BH16 6BB (0202 622222). Small, quiet, grass site for 30 pitches in wooded surroundings off the A350 Blandford to Poole Road. Convenient for ferry crossings from Poole only four miles away. Open Easter to 30th September. SPECIAL OFFER of 25 per cent reduction for five caravans/tents or more in off peak months of April, May, June and September. Caravan Rallies may also be booked for the 1994 season. Covered storage available for boats and caravans.

POOLE near. 💲 Beacon Hill Touring Park, Blandford Road North, Near Poole BH16 6AB (0202

631631). Set in 30 acres of lovely English woodland with open grassy spaces and nature rambles, but only minutes from the South's most beautiful beaches. Beacon Hill offers some of the best facilities available at touring parks today plus the delights of Poole, Bournemouth and Dorset's endless tourist attractions. Facilities include free showers (also disabled facilities), modern toilets, laundry rooms, dishwashing facilities, Calor gas, hair dryers, public telephone and electric hook-ups. Also available is a heated swimming pool, games room, tennis, children's adventure playground, fully licensed bar and shop with off-licence. Fishing on site, two small lakes and riding nearby. Overnight stops for Poole; Cherbourg; Brittany and Channel Island ferries. Only three miles from ferry terminal. Brochure on application.

POOLE near. 🏴 Å **Merley Court Touring Park, Merley, Wimborne, Near Poole BH21 3AA (0202 881488).** Widely recognised as one of the finest and most well-equipped touring parks in Britain, Merley Court was in 1991 named the first ever English Tourist Board "Caravan Park of the Year" and more recently was "Practical Caravan" Magazine's "Best Family Park" Award Winner for 1993. The facilities at Merley Court are extensive and include shop, take-away food bar, licensed club (with family room), games room, outdoor swimming pool, tennis court and adventure playground. Open from 1st March to January 7th each year. A free brochure illustrating the superb facilities is available on request. Touring caravans, tents and motor vans welcome.

RINGWOOD. 🏴 **Oakhill Holiday Park, 234 Ringwood Road, St. Leonards, Ringwood BH24 2SB (0202 876968).** Secluded, quiet 10 acre site situated within 40 acres of private woodland. Clean toilets, showers, hot water to washbasins. Laundry room, hair and hand dryers. Electric hook-ups. Dogs permitted. Dairy produce sold. Touring caravans for hire. Within easy reach of the New Forest and Bournemouth. SAE, please for details. From £3.50 per night, two persons, car, tent.

THE **ULWELL COTTAGE** CARAVAN PARK

ROSE AWARD

AA ▶▶▶

Situated under the Purbeck Hills near the safe and sandy beaches of Swanage and Studland which are suitable for all water sports. There are riding stables and a golf course nearby.

**HEATED INDOOR POOL
FREE SHOWERS & TOILETS
GENERAL STORE
BAR & RESTAURANT
TWO LAUNDERETTES
CHILDREN'S PLAY AREA**

Swanage · Dorset   Telephone: 0929 422823   Proprietors: Mr J. Orchard and Mrs J. Scadden

2 bed vac — (265) 1-3yr — booked
9-16 July 205   4-7yr

BIRCHWOOD
TOURIST · PARK

The newest and probably the finest touring Park in Dorset. Situated in Wareham Forest with direct access to forest walks. Large, level, well drained pitches together with facilities comparable with the best in Europe.

The ideal base for exploring this beautiful part of Dorset.

If, having booked at Birchwood Tourist Park you find the same facilities cheaper anywhere in Dorset we will refund the difference.

Write or phone for colour brochure
BIRCHWOOD TOURIST PARK, NORTH TRIGON,
WAREHAM, DORSET BH20 4DD

0929-554763
The Friendly Touring Park

WARMWELL
COUNTRY TOURING PARK
Warmwell, Nr. Dorchester, Dorset DT2 8JE

Set in 15 acres of natural landscaped grounds, only 7 miles from the sea, in beautiful Hardy countryside.
The park is exclusively for touring caravans, motor-homes and tents. Most of the 190 pitches have electrical hook-ups with a choice of wooded or open sites.

- *Licensed private club*
- *Children's adventure playground and amusements*
- *Showers and hot water facilities included in terms*
- *Dogs on lead accepted*
- *Mini-market*
- *Launderette*
- *Fresh Water Points*
- *Elsan Points*
- *RALLIES WELCOMED*

Just across the road is a major attraction. The facilities are open to the public and include indoor fun pool with wave machine, water flume etc., a dry ski run – lessons available, large bars, nightly entertainment, disco, dancing, children's bar and amusements, sports hall.

OPEN ALL YEAR

FOR A COLOUR BROCHURE: TEL (0305) 8 5 2 3 1 3

WAREHAM. 🏕 Manor Farm Caravan Park, East Stoke, Wareham BH20 6AW (0929 462870). Resident Proprietors: David and Gillian Topp. Flat grass touring park on a working farm in a rural area of outstanding natural beauty, central for most parts of Dorset. Family-run, with clean showers and toilets; play area; shop; 16-AMP hook-ups; gas exchange. Seasonal pitches, winter storage. Dogs by arrangement only and must be kept under STRICT control. AA Three Pennants; RAC Appointed; Caravan and Camping Club Listed. Directions: from Wareham take A352 turning left onto B3070; at first crossroads turn right, second crossroads turn right, and Park is 300 yards on left. For details, send SAE or Dial-a-Brochure. No groups or singles accepted. Also, four-berth caravans for hire.

WEYMOUTH. 🏕 **Pebble Bank Caravan Park, Camp Road, Wyke Regis, Weymouth DT4 9HF (0305 774844).** √ √ √ AA two Pennants. Pebble Bank Caravan Park is situated one and a half miles from Weymouth town centre. The Park is broadly divided into two sections, one for touring vans/campers and recreational space and the other privately owned static holiday vans, some of which are let for holiday bookings. Facilities include numerous water points and electric hook-ups, first class toilet and shower facilities and chemical disposal points, laundry room, children's play area, etc. Dogs allowed provided they are well behaved and kept on leads. Our aim is to give the discerning visitor the most relaxed, comfortable and enjoyable holiday possible. Brochure available.

WIMBORNE. 🏕 Mr and Mrs Peter Arnold, Charris Camping and Caravan Park, Candy's Lane, Corfe Mullen, Wimborne BH21 3EF (Wimborne [0202] 885970). √ √ √ √ A small rural site commanding extensive views over Stour Valley. 45 pitches, some level/sloping. Modern facilities. Personal service. Unspoiled. Ideal for Spring and Autumn breaks in Dorset countryside near coast, New Forest, Purbecks and Cranbourne Chase. National Trust properties within easy reach. Local golf, fishing, riding. Booking advisable July and August. Children and pets welcome. Half-mile western end of Wimborne by-pass A31 follow International signs. Open March to October inclusive. English Tourist Board (Southern) registered. AA 3 Pennant, RAC and Caravan Club Listed, and Camping and Caravan Club Recommended. Terms from £4.50 per night.

Terms quoted in this publication may be subject to increase if rises in costs necessitate

CAMPING SITES

LYME REGIS. ⚠ **Mrs G. Appleton, Uplyme Touring Park, Hook Farm, Gore Lane, Uplyme, Lyme Regis DT7 3UU (0297 442801).** ETB √ √ Peaceful countryside site with beautiful views over the Lyme Valley. Good position for exploring East Devon and West Dorset. Local attractions include clean sandy beaches with safe swimming (two miles), fossil hunting, coastal walks. The seven acre site has 100 pitches on landscaped, terraced and slightly sloping land, with trees providing shelter. New facilities include heated toilet/shower blocks and children's adventure playground. Also available are laundry, shop, pay-phone, electrical hook-ups and bicycle hire. Ready erected tents, self-catering farmhouse and caravan accommodation available. Prices from £6 per pitch per night. Open March 26th — October 31st. SAE, please for brochure. BHHPA, RAC.

DURHAM

CARAVAN SITES AND NIGHT HALTS

ALLENSFORD. 🔣 ⚠ **Allensford Caravan Park, Castleside (0207 591043).** √ √ √ GATEWAY TO THE NORTH PENNINES. An ideal family holiday destination with just that little bit more to offer. Right on the edge of the North Pennines, Allensford provides easy access into the Area of Outstanding Natural Beauty and the Durham Dales. Not only can you get away from it all in an idyllic riverside setting, but it makes a perfect base from which to explore the North East's major attractions — Durham Cathedral, Hadrian's Wall, the Metro Centre, etc. The site itself can accommodate up to 50 vans plus additional pitches for camping and static vans. There is an electric hook-up facility, two toilet blocks, showers and a laundry room. Next to the site is a children's play park and a 14-acre picnic area running alongside the River Derwent. Site shop. Dogs allowed on lead. Open 1st March to 31st October. Brochure.

DURHAM – LAND OF THE PRINCE BISHOPS

From the North Pennine hills and dales in the west to the magnificent Cathedral City at its heart, Durham offers so much to the visitor. Step into the past for a day at the award-winning Beamish Open Air Museum, find out how Victorian lead miners lived and worked at Killhope in Weardale. Castles and ancient churches, market towns and unspoilt villages, England's highest waterfall – there's something for everyone.

BARNARD CASTLE. Mr and Mrs D.S. Peat, Thorpe Hall, Wycliffe, Barnard Castle DL12 9TW (Teesdale [0833] 627230). √ √ √ √ One-and-a-half miles north of A66 near Greta Bridge turning to Wycliffe. Space for 12 touring caravans or motorvans in one-and-a-half acres. Open April to September inclusive. AA Listed, ETB graded. A quiet park in the old walled garden of Thorpe Hall, an 18th century residence built for Christopher Wilkinson, who was Lord of the Manor in 1740. The area is of historic interest and great natural beauty. It is an ideal base for visiting Upper Teesdale, the Durham Dales and the North Yorkshire Dales of Wensleydale, Swaledale, and Arkengarthdale. Durham County was "The Land of the Prince Bishops" who ruled the area for some 800 years, had vice-regal powers and "Lived like Kings". Caravan and two people £7 per night.

BISHOP AUCKLAND. Å Mr J.A. Harker (Manager), The Lambton Estates, Witton Castle, Witton-Le-Wear, Bishop Auckland DL14 0DE (Bookings: Witton-Le-Wear [038-888] 230). Fly fishing offered (migratory fish and rainbow/brown trout) within four miles, also golf, pony trekking and canoeing. The castle (built 1410) is the setting for this touring site. Essential facilities are provided for a modern site without spoiling the medieval tranquillity which lends itself to a holiday site. Castle is also used as a venue for public events on an annual basis: Horse Trials, Point to Points etc. Situated in central Durham within a day's journey of Scottish Borders, Lake District, North Yorkshire Moors, beaches of Northumbria, and the serene beauty of Tyne, Wear and Tees valleys. Signposted, on A68 between Toft Hill and Witton-le-Wear. Children and pets welcome. Tourers and campers from £6 per night. Annual parking £95. Also camping barn and Camping/Caravanning Rally Site. Open April to October.

DURHAM. The Eilands Caravan Park, Landieu, Frosterley (0388 527230). √ √ √ Set between the Weardale village of Wolsingham and Frosterley, this beautifully located park is surrounded by magnificent walking countryside which makes it a superb base for exploring Weardale. Situated on the banks of the River Wear, the site also serves as an ideal spot for any fishing enthusiasts. Enjoy picturesque moorland drives into the Tyne Valley and the market town of Hexham to the north, and to the south a short drive into the Tees Valley to see High Force Waterfall or visit historic Barnard Castle. Site facilities include showers, toilets, mains hook-ups. Overnight tourers welcome. Dogs allowed on lead. Open 1st March to 31st October. Brochure.

STANHOPE. Heather View Caravan Park, Stanhope, Weardale (0388 528728). √ √ √ √ Situated beside the River Wear only a 10 minute walk from Stanhope village. In easy reach of some of the area's most beautiful countryside. Accessible to the Lakes via Alston. Picturesque site ideally positioned for those seeking peace and quiet. Weardale itself is an area of outstanding natural beauty with many attractions such as the Killhope Lead Mining Centre and Allenheads Heritage Centre. Site facilities include toilets, showers with hot and cold water; shop; laundry area, razor and hairdryer points; children's slide and swings. Picturesque country walk to nearby open-air heated swimming pool. Dogs allowed on lead. Seasonal touring pitches available. Open from 1st March to 31st October. Daily rates on application. Brochure.

ESSEX

CARAVANS FOR HIRE

MALDON. 🚐 💲 🏕 **Barrow Marsh, Mill Beach, Maldon CM9 7RA (Maldon [0621] 852859).** Close to Blackwater Estuary. Bus service to Maldon. Caravans for letting from April to October, comprising one double and two single beds, and separate kitchen. One caravan with electricity and gas, the other with just gas for heating, lighting and fridge. Blankets and pillows provided. Toilets, showers, washing machine and water supply close by. Shop 200 yards. Licensed hotel 500 yards. Rates from £30 to £70 per week according to season and caravan (£5 deduction for second consecutive week), or £7 to £15 per night. Deposit £5 per week with bookings. Camping also possible. Tourers welcome. Further details from: **Mrs Hillman.**

CARAVAN SITES AND NIGHT HALTS

COLCHESTER. 💲 🏕 **Mr and Mrs R. Tod, Seven Arches Farm, Chitts Hill, Lexden, Colchester CO3 5SX (0206 574896).** Pleasant, flat, one-acre site, well maintained and with many matured and new trees and shrubs, part of a 100-acre farm overlooking the Colne Valley and the River Colne. Two miles from the oldest recorded town of Colchester, close to the A12 and A604 for Cambridge, Harwich and Constable country. Facilities include toilets, hot showers and washbasins. Site for five touring caravans and tents (£4.50). One static caravan with electricity and £80 per week. Directions: from the A12 take the Cambridge A604, at the first roundabout take the Halstead Road for one mile, turn right at Chitts Hill railway crossing gates.

LOUGHTON. 💲 **Debden House Camp Site, Debden Green, Loughton IG10 2PA (081-508 3008).** 15 miles north of London in Epping Forest, two miles north of Loughton M25 to Junction 26 then A121 (Loughton). Left on to A1168 Rectory Lane, second left Pyries Lane, over crossroads, right on to England's Lane, then second left. Epping Forest is 40 minutes from London. London and East Anglia Tourist Board registered. Electric Sites. Terms from £3.50 (adult), family fee £11. London Borough of Newham residents reduced rates. Open April to October.

ST. LAWRENCE BAY. 💲 🏕 **St. Lawrence Holiday Home Park, 10 Main Road, St. Lawrence Bay CM0 7LY (0621 779434).** √ √ √ Friendly, family-run park (established 1950) offering luxury holiday homes on the River Blackwater. We are renowned for the peace and quiet of the park and have our own private beach and slipway. Probably the best watersports area in Essex. At our "Inn on the Park" catering facilities are available, with a children's room and playground. Contact us now for details of New and Used holiday homes. Pets welcome.

GLOUCESTERSHIRE

CARAVANS FOR HIRE

CRANHAM. 🚐 **Mrs J.P. Whitaker, Overtown Farmhouse, Cranham, Near Gloucester GL4 8HQ (Gloucester [0452] 862573).** Shepherds Piece is a twin unit mobile home with two double bedrooms. It has a lounge with colour TV; kitchen; bathroom and diningroom. Fitted carpets and double glazing. Parking and small garden. Necessary household requisites are supplied except linen and electricity which is metered. Situated adjoining the common and near the nature reserve common woods. There are attractive walks. Cranham is in a good position for touring the Cotswolds. Children and pets welcome. Terms for Shepherds Piece from £55 to £155 per week.

CARAVAN SITES AND NIGHT HALTS

CHELTENHAM. 🏷 Å **Mrs J. Shipway, Longwillows, Station Road, Woodmancote, Cheltenham GL52 4HN (0242 674113).** √ √ √ Situated three and a half miles from Cheltenham Spa, the site is in a sheltered position at the foot of Nottingham Hill and provides an excellent base to explore the Cotswolds. Our well kept facilities include free hot water, showers, washbasins, deep sinks, WCs, razor points, hairdryers and a launderette. We have electric hook-ups, Elsan disposal point, public telephone, facilities for the disabled and a children's playground. There is a pub/restaurant adjoining the site. Dogs are accepted if kept on the lead and we have a dog walking area. The village shops are half a mile away. Licensed for 80 pitches. AA 2 Pennants. Prices from £5.20; one man tents £2.60.

COTSWOLDS. 🏷 **Mrs Joan C. Mitchell, The Red Lion Caravan and Camping Park, Wainlode Hill, Norton, Near Gloucester GL2 9LW (Gloucester [0452] 730251).** Between Gloucester and Tewkesbury on the banks of the lovely River Severn. Three and three-quarter miles north of Gloucester. Turn off A38 at Norton, signposted Wainlode Hill. Running water, hot and cold. Flush toilets, showers, razor points. Laundry. Electric hook-ups. Shop on site, hot and cold food every day, fully licensed. Fishing available on site. Two furnished cottages to let. Car and caravan, Dormobiles, camping from £5 per night. All terms inclusive of VAT.

HAMPSHIRE

CARAVANS FOR HIRE

MILFORD-ON-SEA. 🚐 **Downton Holiday Park, Shorefield Road, Milford-on-Sea SO41 0LH (Tel and Fax: 0425 476131 and 0590 642515).** √ √ √ √

We are on the edge of the New Forest and close to the sea. Green fields are across the country lane from us. We let only 21 luxury caravans on our small, quiet park with shower and colour TV. A shop, laundry and children's play equipment are on premises. Swimming, riding and sailing are all nearby. Bournemouth is about 25 minutes away by car. The Isle of Wight can be reached by ferry from Lymington. We believe our prices which start at £53 per week Low Season are very hard to beat. Please telephone or write for a free brochure.

HOLIDAY PARKS AND CENTRES

See also Colour Display Advertisement **ST. LEONARDS.** 🚐 ☼ 🅂 ⛺ **The Manager, Village Holidays, Oakdene Holiday Park, St. Leonards, Near Ringwood, Hampshire (Ferndown [0202] 875422).** Site with 200 statics and room for 600 tents and tourers. The caravans, eight-berth, are fully equipped and available from March to October. Site has toilets, showers, laundry, shop, licensed bars, games room, children's playground and entertainment nightly in season. Stables. Adjoining local river and close to New Forest. Eight miles from the sea. Easy access off A31. Children welcome and pets allowed. Terms vary according to season.

CARAVAN SITES AND NIGHT HALTS

CHRISTCHURCH. 🟊 **Mrs Mary Latham Frampton, Harrow Wood Farm Caravan Park, Poplar Lane, Bransgore, Christchurch BH23 8JE (Bransgore [0425] 672487).** √ √ √ √ This is a quiet, secluded site bordered by woods and meadows with easy access to New Forest. Four miles from the beach and village shops close by. 60 touring vans, all hard standings, all with electric hook-ups. Showers, toilets, laundry room. Open March to October. Sorry, no pets. On the A35 from Lyndhurst to Christchurch, approximately 11 miles turn right at the "Cat and Fiddle", then approximately one-and-a-half miles to Bransgore and first right after school, you will arrive at this six-acre site. AA 3 Pennants. BH&HPA Member. ETB Listed. Send SAE for brochure.

HAYLING ISLAND. 🟊 🛆 **Lower Tye Camp Site, Copse Lane (0705 462479); The Oven Camp Site, Manor Road (0705 464695); Fleet Farm Camp Site, Yew Tree Road (0705 463684).** Family camping on Hayling Island. Marked sites, parking by units; level and shaded. Hot showers, flush toilets, children's play area, doggie walks, electric hook-ups, fun evenings for children in season. Near pub, shop. Café on site at Lower Tye and Fleet. Hayling Island has good safe beaches, all water sports, excellent windsurfing, golf and fishing. Handy for Portsmouth, Isle of Wight, New Forest, etc. £6 per night two people plus VAT. Caravan storage £3.50 per week plus VAT or permanently on site for £10 per week plus VAT. Special rally field. Follow A3023 from Havant. RAC and AA registered.

See also Colour Display Advertisement **LYMINGTON near.** 🟊 **Shorefield Country Park, Dept GCC, Shorefield Road, Downton, Near Lymington SO41 0LH (0590 642513).** √ √ √ √ Our exclusive touring site at Lytton Lawn is arguably the best holiday location for caravan tourers in Britain. Only two and a half miles from Shorefield Country Park, set in beautiful natural parkland close to Milford beach. Every conceivable leisure facility is on site or close by — sailing, fishing, horse riding, golf, tennis and lots more. Caravans have individual pitches; facilities include electric hook-ups, showers and launderette. Children's play area. Free membership to Shorefield Leisure Club. Rallies welcome. Free brochure available.

NEW FOREST. 🟊 **Forestry Commission, Queen's House, Lyndhurst SO43 7NH (0703 283771).** Camping and Caravanning in the New Forest. A unique opportunity to enjoy a stay in the heart of this historic and beautiful area. The choice of campsites ranges from full facility to very informal; some are in open heathland, others are in woodland. Advance bookings may be made for Hollands Wood, Holmsley, Ashurst and Setthorns. All sites take bookings for Spring Bank Holiday. Electric hook-ups are available at Holmsley and Setthorns. The season runs from the end of March to the end of September with Ashurst campsite remaining open to the end of October; Setthorns is open all year. Information, camping brochure and tariff on request.

ROMSEY. 🟊 🛆 **Eddie and Miriam White, Doctors Hill Farm Caravan and Camping Park, Sherfield English, Romsey SO51 6JX (07943 40402).** √ √ √ The Park is situated half a mile north of the A27, four miles from Romsey. Within easy reach of New Forest, Romsey, Winchester, Salisbury and Southampton. The Park consists of 10 acres of flat and sloping grassland in a quiet rural area, surrounded by woods and fields. Facilities also for touring vans and tents. Amenities include toilet and shower facilities, Calor gas supplies, ice pack service. Terms from £6 per night per unit, i.e., caravan/tent up to two adults and two children; extra child 50p, extra adult £1. Electric hook-ups and awnings extra.

CAMPING SITES

RINGWOOD near. 🛆 **Red Shoot Camping Park, Linwood, Near Ringwood BH24 3QT (Ringwood [0425] 473789).** √ √ √ √ Beautifully situated in the heart of the NEW FOREST, yet only half-hour drive to Bournemouth and coast. Four acres of close mown meadow. Ideal centre for walking and touring and for nature lovers. Pets welcome. Open 1st March to 31st October. *Approved site — tents and caravans *Good toilets and showers *Facilities for disabled *Well stocked shop *Safe playground *Laundry room *Electric hook-ups *Forest inn adjacent — families and dogs welcomed *Owner-managed to high standard. Please send SAE for brochure. From the east, turn off M27 at Exit 1, and follow signs to Linwood. From the west, turn off A338 two miles north of Ringwood, at sign to Linwood. Tourist Board registered.

PLEASE ENCLOSE A STAMPED ADDRESSED ENVELOPE WITH ENQUIRIES

HEREFORD & WORCESTER

CARAVANS FOR HIRE

WYE VALLEY/ROYAL FOREST OF DEAN.

🚐 **Mr M.G. Hawkins, Eastville Caravan Park, Coopers Road, Christchurch, Near Coleford, Gloucestershire BS5 6SR (0272 510082 or 0275 833603).** √ √ √ √ Eastville Caravan Park is a small, quiet site with superb views overlooking the surrounding countryside on B4234 road to Ross-on-Wye. Dogs are not permitted on the site. All caravans for hire have mains services with own toilet, showers, hot and cold water and heating. Free colour TV. Local shops plus extensive sports facilities in area: fishing, pony trekking, canoeing, tennis, golf and many others. Send SAE or telephone for details and terms. Open all year.

KENT

CARAVANS FOR HIRE

HERNE BAY near. 🚐 **Mr and Mrs D. A. Poole, 2 Selwood Cottage, Hoopers Lane, Broomfield, Near Herne Bay CT6 7BP (Canterbury [0227] 374951).** This 26' six-berth Pemberton caravan stands in a sunny position, secluded from house, on a lawn in a large country garden. No restrictions — holidaymakers may come and go as they please. Everything supplied except linen. Gas cooker with oven, fridge, TV, etc. Metered electricity to caravan and personal shower and washroom alongside. Children welcome; pets allowed. Parking space. Sea one-and-a-half miles. An ideal place for visiting resorts by car or bus — peaceful and quiet after a day out. Shop in village. Available Easter to end October. Terms from £55 including gas. SAE, please.

FOLKESTONE near. 🚐 💷 **Varne Ridge Caravan Park, 145 Old Dover Road, Capel-le-Ferne, Near Folkestone CT18 7HX (0303 251765).** Varne Ridge is a small secluded caravan park overlooking the English Channel. Situated at Capel-le-Ferne midway between Folkestone and Dover, it makes the ideal spot for travelling to and from the Continent either by ferry etc, or the Channel Tunnel. All caravans are fully serviced. ETB Rose Award Winners. Units from £75 per week low season, from £95 per week high season. Car and caravan or motor caravan from £5.50 per night. Open 11 months, closed February. SAE please.

HOLIDAY PARKS AND CENTRES

BIRCHINGTON. 🚐 ☼ 💷 ⅄ **Mrs L.D. Sullivan, Two Chimneys Holiday Park, Shottendane Road, Birchington CT7 0HD (Thanet [0843] 41068 or 43157).** √ √ √ √ Our caravan park is a friendly family-run park on a beautiful country site only two miles from the sea. The park has all modern facilities including a licensed club house, tennis court, shop, sauna, spa bath, solarium, heated pools, amusement arcade and children's playground. Ideally situated for visiting the city of Canterbury with its famous cathedral; the popular seaside resorts of Margate, Broadstairs and Ramsgate, best known for their sandy beaches, night clubs and theatres; Bem Bom Brothers Amusement Park and day trip excursions to France: these are only a few of the many attractions around Kent. Terms: Tourers from £5 to £11.50 per night; Holiday Hire from £105 to £350 per week.

FREE and REDUCED RATE Holiday Visits!
Don't miss our Reader's Offer Vouchers on pages 13 to 31.

GET UP AND GO

If you're looking for somewhere to pitch your tent or park your tourer — you need look no further than New Beach Touring Park. Because we're right by the beach and provide the very best amenities for the perfect touring holiday.

You can choose a site with or without electrical hook-up to suit your individual requirements. And, naturally, every site has easy access to mains water, disposal points, gas sales and a modern shower and toilet facilities.

What's more, you can take advantage of all the fabulous **FREE** facilities and entertainment at our Holiday Village next door including: ★ indoor heated pool ★ licensed club bar ★ adult & childrens entertainment ★ launderette ★ ★ supermarket & much much more ★

Reserve your site by calling our Holiday Hotline now!

TOURING HOTLINE
0303 872234

NewBeach
Touring Park

New Walton Pier Co, Walton on the Naze, Essex CO14 8ES

CARAVAN SITES AND NIGHT HALTS

BIDDENDEN. 🔊 Å **Mr R. Jessop, Woodlands Park, Tenterden Road, Biddenden TN27 8BT (0580 291216).** √ √ √ √ Woodlands offers quiet peaceful holidays in beautiful countryside, with castles, gardens, historic houses and pretty villages nearby. The tourist site is level and grassy with a wood down one side and a high hedge to the top end. Amenities include taps, toilets, hot showers, chemical disposal, washing-up room, children's play area, electrical hook-ups, razor points, launderette, Calor and Camping gas sales, camping accessory sales, ice pack freezing, licensed bar. Fishing, new leisure centre with heated indoor swimming pool at Tenterden three miles from park. Biddenden village for shops, restaurants one and a half miles. Open March to October. SAE for terms.

EASTCHURCH. 🔊 **Mr C.V. Spurrier, Warden Springs Caravan Park, Warden Point, Eastchurch, Isle of Sheppey ME12 4HF (0795 880216).** √ √ √ √ DIRECTIONS — M2 turn off junction 5; A249 to Isle of Sheppey. Turn right at roundabout on Sheppey B2231 to Eastchurch and turn left at church. First right to Warden Point. A secluded park set in a privately owned 38-acre estate surrounded by open farmland and overlooking the sea. On-site amenities include clubhouse with two bars and live entertainment, shop, showers, toilets including facilities for disabled visitors, launderette, children's playground, 9-hole pitch and putt course, take-away restaurant and heated outdoor swimming pool. Horse riding, fishing, boating, golf, beautiful cliff-top walks and excellent night entertainment all nearby. Booking advisable. Tourist Board registered.

FOLKESTONE. 🔊 Å **Black Horse Farm Caravan and Camping Park.** √ √ √ √ On A260 Folkestone to Canterbury road at Densole, a rural park of four acres, all tourers. Quiet, no on-park amusements, mostly level grass. Good facilities, shop opposite park entrance. Electric hook-ups. Ideal base for exploring East Kent, Canterbury and for Channel Ferries at Dover and Folkestone. Open all year. From £6.50 per night for caravan/car/two persons. For further information contact: **Pat and Gordon Haddow, 385 Canterbury Road, Densole, Folkestone CT18 7BG (0303 892665).**

RAMSGATE. 🔊 **Mr and Mrs D. Steed, Pine Meadow Caravan Park, Spratling Court Farm, Spratling Street, Manston, Ramsgate CT12 5AN (0843 587770).** √ √ √ √ Directions — turn west (towards Manston) off the A256 onto the B2050 in 500 yards turn right (north) onto farm road. "Practical Caravan" recently featured us and said: "a peaceful attractive park near the seaside resorts of Broadstairs, Ramsgate and Margate". Within the grounds of a Georgian farmhouse surrounded by 350 acres of farmland are 40 pitches all with hook-ups, a late night stop area, play area and excellent shower and loo block. Close to Sally Line for Cross Channel hops. Dogs are not allowed in the park. Rates from £7 per night. Booking recommended. SAE for brochure.

LANCASHIRE

CARAVAN SITES AND NIGHT HALTS

BLACKPOOL. ☼ 🔊 Å **Mrs Barbara Rawcliffe, Pipers Height Caravan and Camping Park, Peel Road, Peel, Blackpool FY4 5JT (Blackpool [0253] 763767).** The site is three miles from Blackpool, near A583, and quarter mile from M55. It accommodates 50 tents, 100 touring caravans and 16 static vans. New static caravan sales. Cottage hire. Booking is advisable in high season. Hot showers. Flush toilets. Power points, also caravan hard stands and electric hook-up points. Site shop. Licensed bar and family room with hot and cold meals served. Children's play area. Take-away food. Launderette. Dogs welcome. Hourly bus service. Facilities available for disabled visitors. Open March-October. Terms from £9 per night. Strictly families only.

BLACKPOOL. 🔊 Å **Mrs P.M. Routledge, Gillett Farm Caravan Park Ltd, Peel Road, Peel, Blackpool FY4 5JU (0253 761676).** √ √ √ √ Caravan and camping site three miles from Blackpool, three miles from Lytham and three and a half miles from St. Annes. Only 900 yards from M55 motorway, Exit 4. Turn left onto A583. 400 yards traffic lights turn right and immediately left into Peel Road. Site second on right, 350 yards. Golf, fishing and water ski-ing are available in the area. The site has many amenities: toilets, hot and cold showers, chemical toilet disposal, shaver and hairdryer points, launderette with dryer, ironing room, and public telephone. Camp shop open 8.15 a.m. to 10 p.m. Take-away meals available. TV and games room. Mains electric hook-ups. Hard standings. Gas cylinders exchanged. Children welcome. Dogs must be kept on lead. Terms £5 to £11.

LITTLEBOROUGH. 🔊 Å **Mr F. Mills, Hollingworth Lake Caravan Park, Round House Farm, Rakewood, Littleborough OL15 0AT (0706 378661).** Situated in local beauty spot overlooking lake, adjacent to Country Park. Local attractions within one mile include fishing, boating, sailing, and small paddle boats. Amusements for children. Ideally situated for hill walking, being near the Pennine Way and Roman Road. Pony trekking from the Park. Hot and cold showers, razor points, WCs, and laundry. From £5 per night. Electric hook-ups £1.50. Sites for caravans and tents. Directions: off A58, follow Hollingworth Lake Country Park signs to the Fish Hotel, take Rakewood Road. Second on right.

RIVERSIDE
LEISURE CENTRE
TOURING AND CAMPING PARK

**Southport New Road, Banks, Southport
Lancashire PR9 8DF   Tel: 0704 28886   Fax: 0704 505886**

Situated on A565 – Unrivalled Facilities for Entertainment

* Theme Nights: 'Country and Western' and 'Back to the 60's Era';
* Live Music and Discos; * New Games Room and Discos for Children;
* Hot and Cold Showers; * General Store; * Play Areas; * Launderette;
* Electric Hook-ups; * Calor and Camping Gaz stockist; * Fishing;
* Dogs allowed; * Fish and Chip Shop; * Fishing available.

*The park is set in acres of pleasant meadowland with trees providing
adequate wind-breaks; hard standing available.*

LINCOLNSHIRE

CARAVAN SITES AND NIGHT HALTS

BOSTON. 🏕 Ⓐ **Mrs Kibby, The White Cat Caravan Park, Shaw Lane, Old Leake, Boston PE22 9LQ (Old Leake [0205] 870121).** The park of two-and-a-half acres is situated in quiet, rural surroundings and can be found eight miles outside Boston on the A52 Skegness road. Turn right opposite the B1184 Sibsey road. The park is 300 yards on the left. Flush toilets, handbasins, H&C, chemical disposal point, free showers, washroom, razor points, electric hook-ups, site shop and children's swings. Dogs allowed. Public houses and restaurants nearby. £3.75 per night for low season rising to £4.75 high season. Six-berth caravans for hire from £73 per week. Open March-November, ideal for touring and fishing, AA 3 Pennant site. Further details on request.

NORFOLK

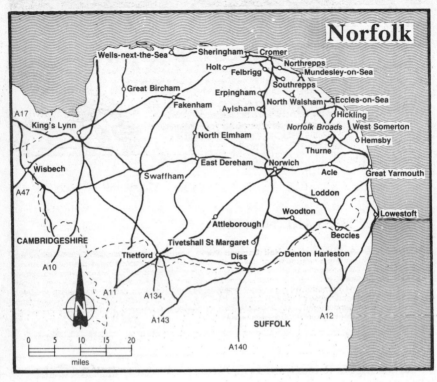

CARAVANS FOR HIRE

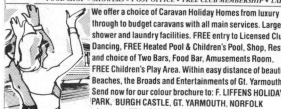

CARAVAN SITES AND NIGHT HALTS

CAWSTON. 🔟 **Å Haveringland Hall Caravan Park, Cawston, Norwich NR10 4PN (Norwich [0603] 871302).** Formerly the grounds of Haveringland Hall, the Park is noted for its beautiful specimen trees. The 12-acre lake stocked with coarse fish is very popular with anglers. The Park is ideally situated for touring Norfolk, being 10 miles from Norwich and the Broads, and only 17 miles from the sea. Sandringham, King's Lynn and Great Yarmouth are within easy motoring distance. There are sections for touring caravans, tents and seasonal homes. Also holiday caravans for hire. The Park is of special appeal to country lovers and anglers looking for complete seclusion. It has all modern amenities. Terms from £5 to £6 including VAT per night. SAE for brochure to **Ken Rustidge (Manager).**

GREAT YARMOUTH. 🔟 **The Grange Touring Park, Ormesby St. Margaret, Great Yarmouth NR29 3QG (Great Yarmouth [0493] 730306)/730023).** ✔ ✔ ✔ ✔ ✔ A level, grassy park accommodating 70 touring outfits or tents, adjoining the grounds of the Grange Free House, an 18th century building, licensed and selling wide range of beers and real ale. Five minutes' drive from Great Yarmouth at A149 and B1159 junction. One mile from beach. Children's room, amusements and pets corner. Daily mobile shop in high season. Shops half mile away. On-site facilities include mains electricity, modern tiled toilet block, coin-operated washers and dryers, free hot showers, chemical toilet disposal point, all-night lighting and payphone. Convenient for touring Norfolk Broads, historic cathedral city of Norwich, Caister Castle and Motor Museum, Wildlife Gardens. Terms £6.00–£10.00 per night. RAC approved.

GREAT YARMOUTH. 🚐 🔟 **Å Mr A. L. Gage, Wild Duck Chalet, Caravan and Camping Park, Howards Common, Belton, Great Yarmouth NR31 9NE (Great Yarmouth [0493] 780268).** ✔ ✔ ✔ ✔ ✔ One of Norfolk's most delightful parks, set amidst restful pine and wooded countryside with all amenities, toilets, showers, swimming pool, shop, licensed club with entertainment. Electric hook-ups available. Lounge bar for quiet drink and game of darts. Games room. Conveniently situated for Yarmouth and Gorleston beaches, the Broads, fishing etc. New caravans with showers, toilets etc., chalets with bathroom — all six-berth. Children welcome; pets allowed. Caravans and Chalets from £70 to £250. Tourers and campers from £4 to £9 per night. Open from April to October. ETB registered. Rose Award 1993.

GREAT YARMOUTH. 🖼 **Long Beach Estate, Hemsby, Great Yarmouth NR29 4JD (0493 730023).** This private site includes part of Winterton Great Valley and over 40 acres of rolling sand dunes and a fine sandy beach. Peaceful surroundings with walks to the Nature Reserve. Within easy reach of the amusements at Hemsby Gap and only five miles from Great Yarmouth. Convenient for Norwich and the Norfolk Broads. Facilities on site include electric hook-ups, constant hot water, free showers, laundry, children's play area, licensed bar, supermarket, etc. Please write or phone for brochure.

GREAT YARMOUTH near. 🖼 Å **Bureside Holiday Park, Boundary Farm, Oby, Near Great Yarmouth NR29 3BW (0493 369233).** Come to Bureside Holiday Park, a spacious site for touring caravans and tents, and you won't want to leave the peace and tranquillity of its open and unspoilt Broadland. Relax with your family and enjoy the heated swimming pool and kiddies' paddling pool, and evening walks along quiet country lanes and riverbanks. Or, if you prefer a more restful time, hide away with a fishing rod by our own private lake, or launch a boat from on-site slipway. Trekking stables, wildlife parks, beaches and the beautiful cathedral city of Norwich are all within easy reach. Excellent standards of cleanliness and hygiene maintained at all times. Well stocked shop. Open Spring Bank Holiday to mid-September.

MUNDESLEY. 🚐 🖼 **Mrs Williams, Sandy Gulls Caravan Park Ltd., Cromer Road, Mundesley NR11 8DF (Mundesley [0263] 720513).** √ √ √ A safe

cliff top location, miles of clean sandy beaches. Managed by the owning family, the park is gently sloping to ensure good sea views to all visitors. All pitches given plenty of personal space from their all-grass pitches. 40 pitches with hook-ups. Suitable for disabled visitors. New hot showers. Shop nearby. Golf (three courses), fishing (sea and fresh water), horse riding close by. Norfolk Broads 10 miles, Great Yarmouth 30 miles, Cromer five miles, Sheringham nine miles and Norwich 24 miles.

SANDRINGHAM near. 🖼 Å A quiet family run site, 16 acres with an eight-acre lake. Most of the caravans and tents overlook the lake. Showers, toilet facilities; electric hook-ups. Sailing, boating, coarse fishing and bar available. Sandringham House two and a half miles, Hunstanton 15 miles. This is an ideal site for a base for touring Norfolk. Open April to October. For further details contact: **James and Carolyn Donaldson, Gatton Waters Touring Caravan and Camping Site, Hillington, King's Lynn (0485 600643).**

SNETTISHAM. 🚐 💲 🛆 **Diglea Caravan and Camping Park, Beach Road, Snettisham PE31 7RB (Dersingham [0485] 541367).** Attractive level grassed site, quarter-mile from beach and nature reserve, for 200 tents, tourers and motor vans. From King's Lynn take the A149 Hunstanton road to Snettisham. Turn left at sign for Snettisham Beach. Site on left within one and a half miles. Close proximity to Sandringham, Hunstanton, Norfolk Lavender, Thursford Organs and many other places of interest. Facilities on site include electric hook-up points, toilets, showers, chemical disposal point, clubhouse, children's play area, public telephone. Dogs welcome on lead. East Anglian and English Tourist Board registered. AA three pennants and RAC listed. Terms from £5 per night.

NORTHUMBERLAND

CARAVANS FOR HIRE

CORBRIDGE. 🚐 **Mr F.J. Matthews, The Hayes, Newcastle Road, Corbridge NE45 5LP (0434 632010).** Spacious caravan, three self catering cottages and a flat. Also available, attractive stone-built Guest House set in seven acres of grounds. Single, double, twin and family bedrooms; lounge and dining rooms. Available 12 months of the year. Bed and Breakfast £16. Children's reductions. Stair lift for disabled guests. Awarded Three Farm Holiday Guide Diplomas. Car parking. For brochure or booking, please phone or send SAE. ETB registered.

CARAVAN SITES AND NIGHT HALTS

BERWICK-UPON-TWEED. 🏕 ⛺ **Beachcomber House, Goswick, Berwick-upon-Tweed TD15 2RQ (0289 81217).** √ √ √ We have a small site in a remote spot on the sand dunes overlooking Goswick Sands, with direct beach access. We run a quiet, unsophisticated site and offer the best quality site facilities. We have a shower and toilet block with laundry, a small café/bar with glorious views over the Cheviot Hills, and a camp shop stocking basic groceries. We are situated halfway between Berwick and Holy Island, and so offer an ideal base from which to visit all the attractions of northern Northumberland and the Borders. For bookings or more information call **Sue or Julie.**

Seafield Caravan Park
√ √ √

Seafield Road, Seahouses, NE68 7SP
Telephone: 0665 720628 Fax: 0665 720088

NO CARAVANS FOR HIRE

Immaculate grassy park in superb seafront setting overlooking the Farne Islands. Within walking distance of all village amenities, harbour, fishing and sailing. Golf courses nearby. All electric pitches, laundry with dryers and recently refurbished shower, bath and toilet blocks. Dogs welcome under control. Please write or telephone for brochure

NOTTINGHAMSHIRE

CARAVAN SITES AND NIGHT HALTS

WORKSOP. 🏕 ⛺ **Bob and Hazel Hurst, Riverside Caravan Park, Worksop Cricket Club, Central Avenue, Worksop S80 1ER (0909 474118).** √ √ √ √ √ A level grassy park surrounded by trees, part hard standing. Coarse fishing available adjacent. Secluded yet within a few minutes of the town centre. There are 45 pitches on four and a half acres, with electric hook-ups for 26. Showers, toilets, waste disposal on site. Clubhouse belonging to the cricket club adjoining. Closed February only. Pets welcome. Terms from £4 per night.

CARAVAN SITES AND NIGHT HALTS

CALVERTON. 🚐 🏕 **Moor Farm Holiday & Home Park, Calverton NG14 6ZF (0602 652426 & 204695; 0831 839686).** Our Park is set in Nottinghamshire countryside overlooking lakes, five miles north of Nottingham City and close to Sherwood Forest. Facilities nearby include fishing, golf course, restaurant with fruit picking and beautiful country walks. Site amenities include level park, electric hook-ups and caravans for hire. Pets welcome. Terms from £175 per week.

NOTTINGHAMSHIRE – ROBIN HOOD COUNTRY!
Sherwood Forest is now a country park and is one of Nottinghamshire's leading attractions. This county is rich in terms of its parks. There are others at Burntstump, Clumber, Holme Pierrepont and Rufford. Nottingham itself is a surprisingly attractive city.

OXFORDSHIRE

HOLIDAY PARKS AND CENTRES

SHROPSHIRE

CARAVANS FOR HIRE

LUDLOW near. 💰 🏕 **Mrs S.E. Jones, Sparchford Farm, Culmington, Near Ludlow (058473 222).** Secluded site for 10 caravans plus tents, on 250-acre stock farm. Situated in the beautiful Corvedale Valley, ideal for walking, cycling and touring the Ironbridge museums and South Shropshire. Only a short drive from historic Ludlow with its castle, golf and race courses. Milk and bread to order, also home-made cakes, ice cream and fruit in season from the farmhouse. Permits available for fishing the River Corve bordering the farm, also just a short drive from Delbury Hall Trout Fishery. Water, chemical disposal on site, toilet available for campers. Children and pets welcome. Rallies welcome. Prices from £2.

CARAVAN SITES AND NIGHT HALTS

BRIDGNORTH. 💰 🏕 **Stanmore Hall Touring Park, Stourbridge Road, Bridgnorth WV15 6DT (0746 761761).** √ √ √ A458 to Stourbridge, two miles from Bridgnorth. Situated around a lake in mature parkland. Accommodation for 120 units. Ideal centre for visiting historic Bridgnorth, Severn Valley Railway, Ironbridge Gorge and Museums; Cosford Aerospace Museum and many other visitor attractions within easy reach, all in the "Heart of Shropshire". On site are superb new facilities for the 1994 season. All weather "Gold" pitches serviced with water, drainage, electricity and TV (Satellite TV available as an optional extra). "Gold" pitch fees from £10.14 off peak which includes two adults and fully serviced pitch. "Bronze" pitch fees from £7.89 off peak which includes two adults and electric hook-ups. Please send for our FREE colour brochure.

SOMERSET

CARAVANS FOR HIRE

WIVELISCOMBE. **Richard and Marian Rottenbury, Oxenleaze Farm Caravans, Chipstable, Wiveliscombe TA4 2QH (0984 623427).** √ √ √ √ This very picturesque and peaceful site is situated on the Devon/Somerset borders, close to Exmoor amongst some beautiful countryside. Eleven luxury caravans stand on one acre of a working hill farm. Each caravan has its own shower and flush toilet, hot and cold water, cooker, fridge, fire and colour TV. Parking beside each caravan. Car essential. The site offers games room, children's play area with sandpit and swings; there is a barbecue, heated indoor swimming pool, laundry room, telephone and for keen coarse anglers, free fishing, a fisherman's paradise: one and a half acre ponds stocked with large carp and tench. No closed season. Strictly no pets. Early booking advised. Stamp for colour brochure. Open Easter to end October.

Please mention this guide when you write or phone to enquire about accommodation.

If you are writing, a stamped, addressed envelope is always appreciated.

HOLIDAY PARKS AND CENTRES

BREAN SANDS. 🚐 ☼ $ Å **Unity Farm Holiday Centre, Coast Road, Brean Sands TA8 2RB (0278 751235; Fax: 0278 751539).** √ √ √ Try Unity Farm for a super, fun-packed, water splashing, roller coaster, caravan and camping holiday. Situated in 200 acres of level meadowland, only a sand dune away from Brean Sands, with views over open countryside towards Cheddar. The Park accepts tents, touring caravans, motor homes and has holiday homes for hire and for sale. Facilities include an indoor and outdoor pool complex with giant waterslides, an 18-hole golf course, funfair with over 30 attractions, fishing lake, pony trekking, bars with entertainment and a children's Piglet Club. Terms on request. Special Offers in June and September. **Dial a Colour Brochure.**

CARAVAN SITES AND NIGHT HALTS

CHEDDAR. $ Å **Froglands Farm Caravan and Camping Park, Cheddar BS27 3RH (0934 742058).** Small family site situated in a designated area of outstanding natural beauty on A371 Wells/Weston-super-Mare road, close to church, shops, banks, post office, library and swimming pool. Within walking distance of Cheddar Gorge and Caves. 60 touring pitches, electric points, flush toilets, washbasins, showers, shaving points. Shop (Gaz and Calor), Elsan disposal point, launderette, washing-up area. Adjoining field available for rallies. Children and pets welcome. Open Easter to October. SAE for charges. AA Three Pennants.

MARTOCK. 🚐 💲 🏕 **Mrs S. Metcalfe, Southfork Caravan Park, Parrett Works, Martock TA12 6AE (0935 825661; Fax: 0935 825122).** ✓ ✓ ✓ ✓ ✓ Small, family-run "Excellent" graded touring park in beautiful countryside close to River Parrett. Level, grassy site with clean, modern toilet block and laundry room and free hot showers. Play area, grocery shop and off-licence, caravan spares and accessories shop, caravan servicing and repair centre. Numerous places of interest nearby for all age groups, an ideal base for touring. 30 touring pitches, electrical hook-ups, two luxury static holiday caravans for hire. AA Three Pennants, RAC Appointed; member of BH&HPA and National Caravan Council. For further details please contact **Sue and Steve Metcalfe.**

TAUNTON. 🚐 💲 🏕 **Mr and Mrs D.A. Small, Ashe Farm Caravan and Camping Site, Thornfalcon, Taunton TA3 5NW (Henlade [0823] 442567).** ✓ ✓ ✓ In the vale of Taunton Deane, quiet farm site, with 30 touring pitches and two holiday caravans. Sheltered mowed meadow with easy access, quarter-mile off A358, four miles south-east of Taunton. Showers, toilets, hot water, deep sinks, spin dryer, shaver points, electric hook-ups, telephone and daily delivery of farm produce. Pets welcome. Ideal touring site, within easy reach of North and South coasts and Quantock and Blackdown Hills, Exmoor and the Somerset Levels. The fully equipped holiday caravans sleep six. Open April-October. £2.50 per person, £1 children. £1.30 electricity. From M5 Junction 25, take A358 for two-and-a-half miles, then turn right at "Nags Head".

STAFFORDSHIRE

CARAVAN SITES AND NIGHT HALTS

COTTON. 💲 ⛺ **Star Caravan Park, Cotton, Near Alton Towers, Stoke-on-Trent ST10 3DW (0538 702256/702219/308530).** √ √ √ Situated off the B5417 road, between Leek and Cheadle, within 10 miles of the market towns of Ashbourne and Uttoxeter, with Alton Towers just three-quarters of a mile away. A family-run site where your enjoyment is our main concern. Site amenities include large children's play area, shop, toilet block with showers, etc., laundry room with drying and ironing facilities, electric hook-ups, etc. Dogs welcome but must be kept on leash. Open 1st February to 31st December. £4.50 per night for two persons. Special rates for groups and parties of campers (Scouts, schools, etc.) AA two stars. Brochure and further details available.

CAMPING SITES

CANNOCK FOREST (TACKEROO). 🅂 **Forestry Commission, Lady Hill, Birches Valley, Rugeley WS15 2UQ (0889 586593).** Forestry Commission woodland touring caravan site, class 'B', in the heart of Cannock Forest. Well situated as a stop for tourists travelling north or south and an ideal base for exploring the Midlands and the Potteries. Open all year. Rallies by arrangement. Situated in the centre of Cannock Chase off the Rugeley to Penkridge Road. Leave M6 at Junction 14(N) or 11(S). Basic facilities, water and Elsan disposal. SAE or telephone for further information.

SUFFOLK

CARAVANS FOR HIRE

DUNWICH. 📺 ☀ 🅂 🏕 **Cliff House, Minsmere Road, Dunwich IP17 3DQ (Westleton [072873] 282).** √ √ √ Between Aldeburgh and Southwold, adjoining the famous National Trust Minsmere Bird Reserves. Convenient for Aldeburgh Festival. A mature woodland park offering peaceful seclusion in area of outstanding beauty, with its own access to beach. We offer a bar and restaurant, a shop, TV room and a games room. Also on site are showers, electric hook-ups, toilets and a laundry room. Modern static caravans for hire, from four to seven berths with all facilities. Terms from £95 per week, and touring pitches from £7 per unit per night. Open from March to October. New timber chalets/static caravans for sale.

SAXMUNDHAM. 📺 **Mrs Ann Ratcliffe, Fir Tree Farm, Kelsale, Saxmundham, Suffolk IP17 2RH (0728 668356).** Fir Tree Farm dates from Tudor times and stands in 7 acres of fields and gardens. There is a resident moorhen on the pond. A 22 ft. 6-berth caravan is situated in a secluded position. The caravan has mains water and electricity with Calor gas cooker and fire. Chemical toilet in the caravan, flush toilet about 40 yards. Everything provided except linen. Well-behaved pets allowed. Aldeburgh and Southwold 10 miles. Minsmere Bird Sanctuary and Dunwich Beach 10 minutes; wild life parks, castles and Sports Centre with indoor swimming pool nearby. Yoxford with its Pottery, Art-gallery, crafts and several pubs and restaurants is 1 mile. Also self-catering flat in the house available. SAE please or telephone.

CARAVAN SITES AND NIGHT HALTS

LOWESTOFT. 🅂 🏕 **Azure Seas Caravan Park, The Street, Corton, Near Lowestoft (0502 731403 warden; 0493 730023 admin).** Azure Seas is an attractive wooded cliff top site adjoining the beach in the village of Corton just two miles north of Lowestoft and six miles south of Great Yarmouth. Convenient for touring North Suffolk, the Yarmouth area, the Norfolk Broads and the historic cathedral city of Norwich. The popular well known Pleasurewood Hills American Theme Park is very close by. Facilities on site include electric hook-ups, coin-operated laundry, free showers, etc. Shops, licensed bar, swimming pool, etc. are only a short walk away. Please write or phone for brochure.

LOWESTOFT. 🅂 🏕 **North Denes Caravan and Camping Site, Lowestoft NR32 1UX (0502 573197).** Situated between the sea and Sparrows Nest Gardens. Flush toilet and shower blocks, Elsan disposal, launderette, shop, fish and chip shop, bar and restaurant; bowls, tennis and putting green. Site open 1st April to mid-October. THE MOST EASTERLY SITE IN GREAT BRITAIN.

CAMPING SITES

SUDBURY. 🄢 🜉 **Mrs A. Wilson, Willowmere Camping Park, Bures Road, Sudbury CO10 0NN (Sudbury [0787] 375559).** √ √ √ √ This neat little site could be suitable for a weekend or as a touring base for inland Suffolk. It has just 40 pitches, 24 with electric points. Site has single toilet block of good quality and well maintained, with free hot water in the washbasins and showers. No other on-site amenities apart from milk, cold drinks etc. Village shops half a mile away. Open Easter to October. AA, HPA. Terms per unit with two persons from £7.00.

SURREY

CARAVAN SITES AND NIGHT HALTS

FARNHAM. 🄢 🜉 **Tilford Touring Caravan & Camping Park, Tilford, Farnham GU10 2DF (0252 793296).** 75-pitch, secluded, peaceful, very dry level site amidst 1,000 acres of picturesque Hankley Common. Dog loving walkers and mature children welcome. Adjoins championship golf course, with lovely country pub, the DUKE OF CAMBRIDGE adjacent, avoiding drinking and driving worries. Super modern hot showers, electric hook-ups and pay-phone. M25 only 25 minutes away and LONDON just over the hour with all its attractions and shows. Catering particularly for business/workmen who find hotel and bed and breakfast charges expensive. Open all year round. £5 per night, £25 per week. Opportunities exist to leave and use own touring caravan throughout the year for just £10 per week — not residential.

EAST SUSSEX

CARAVAN SITES AND NIGHT HALTS

BODIAM. 🄢 🜉 **Mr Richard Bailey, Park Farm Caravan and Camping Site, Park Farm, Bodiam TN32 5XA (0580 830514).** Quiet rural site in beautiful setting. Off B2244, signposted. Hot showers; children's play area. Barbecues permitted. Riverside walk to Bodiam Castle. Free fishing in River Rother. Open Easter to October. Dogs allowed. Charges: 50p child, £5 per night two adults with caravan or large tent. £2 per person ridge tent. Undercover winter storage available at £5 per week.

HASTINGS. 🄢 🜉 **Whydown Farm Touring Caravan Park, Crazy Lane, Sedlescombe, Hastings**

TN33 0QT (0424 870147). √ √ √ A small secluded family park situated in a sun trap valley in the heart of 1066 country, within easy reach of beaches and all historical sites. Sailing, horse-riding, golf, tennis and fishing facilities are all in easy reach. First class luxury toilet facilities. All pitches individually numbered. 26 touring, 20 motor caravan, 20 electrical hook-up points. Hardstanding for disabled with own fully equipped toilet facility. Dogs are welcome on a lead. Open 1st March — 31st October. From £6.25 per night; book for seven nights, only pay for six! Directions — travelling south of A21 turn left 100 yards past Junction B2244 opposite Blackbrooks Garden Centre, into Crazy Lane, site 70 yards on right.

🚐 Caravans for Hire (one or more caravans for hire on a site)

☼ Holiday Parks & Centres (usually larger sites hiring holiday homes/vans, with amenities)

🄢 Caravan Sites (for touring caravans, caravanettes, etc.)

🜉 Camping Sites (where campers are welcome)

WEST SUSSEX

HOLIDAY PARKS AND CENTRES

CARAVAN SITES AND NIGHT HALTS

ARUNDEL. Maynard's Caravan and Camping Park, Crossbush, Arundel BN18 9PQ (0903 882075). √ √ √ From Arundel on A27 to Worthing or Brighton turn right onto A284 Littlehampton Road, turn into car park behind Howards Hotel, signposted from Arundel. Open all year. £7.00 for two persons including unit, car and hot showers. Electric hook-ups, telephone, children's play area on site. Restaurant and village pub adjacent site. Dogs by arrangement. Places to visit include Arundel Castle and Wild Fowl Reserve, Littlehampton beach, Sussex Downs and Goodwood Racecourse. Leisure pursuits in the area include sailing, fishing, golf, etc. AA 3 Pennants. RAC. BH&HPA. Caravan Club. British Tourist Board.

SELSEY. Warner Farm Touring Park, Warner Lane, Selsey PO20 9EL (0243 604121). √ √ √ √ √ A modern park opened in July 1991 with first class toilet facilities, offering Standard, Electric and Super Pitches. Two swimming pools, one outdoor and one indoor, first class entertainment with three clubs. Shop, launderette, boat hire and sea fishing. All pitches are individually marked and numbered. Situated close to places of interest, e.g., Portsmouth, Arundel, Brighton, etc. AA 4 Pennants awarded. Write or phone for terms.

CAMPING SITES

CHICHESTER. Wicks Farm Caravan Park, Redlands Lane, West Wittering, Chichester PO20 8QD (Birdham [0243] 513116). √ √ √ √ √ Camping Park for tents and motor caravans. Peaceful, rural site with modern toilets, showers and laundry room, with a number of "Electric Pitches". Situated just off the B2179, one mile from the sandy beach of West Wittering, one mile from Chichester harbour at Itchenor. The park is ideally placed for a coastal holiday but within easy reach of many places of interest, including Chichester, Portsmouth and the South Downs. Children and pets welcome. AA and RAC Listed.

TYNE & WEAR

CARAVANS FOR HIRE

SOUTH TYNESIDE. 🚐 💲 Å **Sandhaven Caravan Park.** When visiting South Tyneside why not make use of the excellent facilities available at Sandhaven Caravan Park, and also at our Lizard Lane Caravan Park. Both parks are adjacent to superb sandy beaches and offer you excellent facilities — standage available for statics, tourers and tents, luxurious shower and toilet facilities (including shaver and hair dryer points), electric hook-ups (Sandhaven only), full gas and gaz service. Pets allowed on site (under control). All this and only minutes from the town centre and our rapid transport system, the Tyneside Metro. Whether you prefer simply to relax or discover the surrounding country-side remember SOUTH TYNESIDE HAS IT ALL. Further details contact: **Tourist Information, Cultural and Leisure Activities Dept, Central Library, South Shields, Tyne and Wear (091 427 1818 extension 2030).**

CARAVAN SITES AND NIGHT HALTS

SOUTH TYNESIDE. 💲 Å **Sandhaven Caravan Park.** When visiting South Tyneside why not make use of the excellent facilities available at Sandhaven Caravan Park, and also at our Lizard Lane Caravan Park. Both parks are adjacent to superb sandy beaches and offer you excellent facilities — standage available for statics, tourers and tents, luxurious shower and toilet facilities (including shaver and hair dryer points), electric hook-ups (Sandhaven only), full gas and gaz service. Pets allowed on site (under control). All this and only minutes from the town centre and our rapid transport system, the Tyneside Metro. Whether you prefer simply to relax or discover the surrounding countryside remember SOUTH TYNESIDE HAS IT ALL. Further details contact: **Tourist Information, Cultural and Leisure Activities Dept, Central Library, South Shields, Tyne and Wear (091 427 1818 extension 2030).**

WARWICKSHIRE

CARAVAN SITES AND NIGHT HALTS

HASELEY KNOB, near Warwick. 🅂 **David Clapp, The Croft, Haseley Knob, Warwick CV35 7NL (Tel or Fax: 0926 484447).** Flat, level, well maintained grassy site with some hardstandings. Open all year. Some electric hook-ups (£1.50 per night). Chemical disposal point and water on site. Shower and toilets planned for 1994 — check when booking. From £4.00 per night per van. Campervans, children and pets (if kept under control) welcome. Also B&B and mobile home to let. On the A4177 about 5 miles north west of Warwick towards Balsall Common. Convenient for Warwick, Stratford, Coventry, National Exhibition Centre, National Agricultural Centre (Royal Show), Birmingham Airport and National Motorcycle Museum, all about 15 minutes by car. Birmingham 30 minutes.

STRATFORD-UPON-AVON. 🅂 Å **Mrs M.J. Reading, The Elms Camp, Tiddington Road, Stratford-upon-Avon CV37 7AG (0789 292312 or 293356).** Stratford-upon-Avon one and a half miles. On B4086 Wellesbourne/Stratford. Terms for caravans and tent pitches from £5.50 per night, including VAT. Warwick, NEC, Royal Showground, Cotswolds and the Vale of Evesham are all within easy driving distance; golf course quarter of a mile away, bowling club at site entrance. Gliding, fishing, boating and horse riding are all nearby. Many picturesque pubs and restaurants in the locality for lunches and dinners. Ideal for theatre visits. Limited number of hook-ups available, £2.00 extra charge.

STRATFORD-UPON-AVON. 🅂 Å **Dodwell Park, Evesham Road (B439), Stratford-upon-Avon CV37 9ST (0789 204957).** √ √ √ √ A small touring park, very clean and fairly quiet, set in the countryside two miles south-west of Stratford-upon-Avon. An ideal location from which to visit Shakespeare's birthplace, Anne Hathaway's Cottage, Warwick Castle and the Cotswolds. The park has a well-provisioned shop with off-licence and gas supplies, a launderette and plenty of 10 amp hook-ups. There are country walks to the River Avon and the village of Luddington. From Stratford-upon-Avon take the B439 (formerly A439) towards Bidford-on-Avon for two miles. The park lies on the left, signposted. Open all year. Free brochure on request.

WILTSHIRE

CARAVANS FOR HIRE

DEVIZES. 🚐 Å **Colin and Cynthia Fletcher, Lower Foxhangers Farm, Rowde, Devizes SN10 1SS (Devizes [0380] 828254).** Colin and Cynthia Fletcher invite you to enjoy a country holiday at Lower Foxhangers where we have three large mobile homes for hire in our farm orchard — a quiet sheltered site sloping down to the Kennet and Avon canal. Each home has a lounge with colour TV; fully fitted kitchen, with fridge; airing cupboard; bathroom and two/three bedrooms to sleep four in comfort. A paved patio is provided — no steps to climb. Ideal walking, fishing, also riding, swimming nearby. Easy reach Bath, Longleat, Avebury. Children and pets welcome. £140 to £195 per week. Free gas, electricity, parking. Leaflet by return. Also campsite from £5 per night. Electric hook-ups £1 per night extra.

CARAVAN SITES AND NIGHT HALTS

SALISBURY near. 🅂 Å **Alderbury Caravan and Camping Park, Old Southampton Road, Whaddon, Near Salisbury (0831 380226).** Situated three miles from Salisbury, take A36 to Southampton and turn right for Alderbury. A brand new clean and pleasant site on the edge of a village, close to well stocked local shop and opposite pretty village inn serving excellent food. Site facilities include hot and cold showers, toilets, laundry room, electric hook-ups, telephone. Excellent location for Stonehenge, the New Forest, Broadlands and Bournemouth. Historic Salisbury's wonderful cathedral has the tallest spire in the country (404 ft); visit the open air market on Tuesdays and Saturdays, or walk along the banks of the River Avon. Open Easter to October 31st. No booking necessary.

YORKSHIRE

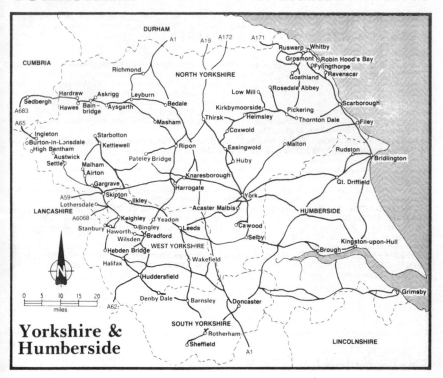

**Yorkshire &
Humberside**

EAST YORKSHIRE

HOLIDAY PARKS AND CENTRES

BRIDLINGTON. 🚐 ☼ **Shirley Caravan Park, Jewison Lane, Sewerby, Bridlington (0262 676442).** √ √ √ Attractively and spaciously laid out, this holiday park is ideally situated for walking the picturesque coastline of famous Flamborough Head. Only a few minutes' drive away lies the seaside holiday town of Bridlington with its picturesque fishing harbour, glorious sandy beaches and numerous other attractions. Site facilities include showers, toilets and laundry with hot and cold water; self-service shop including off-licence; swings and slides etc; lounge bar, games room, family room. Holiday mains serviced units available for hire, weekly rates on application. Seasonal touring pitches available. Dogs allowed on leads. Open 1st March to 30th November. Brochure.

🚐 Caravans for Hire (one or more caravans for hire on a site)

☼ Holiday Parks & Centres (usually larger sites hiring holiday homes/vans, with amenities)

ⓢ Caravan Sites (for touring caravans, caravanettes, etc.)

⚠ Camping Sites (where campers are welcome)

CARAVAN SITES AND NIGHT HALTS

SOUTH CAVE. Waudby's Caravan and Camping Park, Brough Road, South Cave HU15 2DB (0430 422523). Clean family site situated in the picturesque Yorkshire Wolds. Beverley, Hull and York within close driving distance. Large modern toilet and shower facilities, electric hook-ups. Calor Gas and Camping Gaz sales. Disabled facilities. Pets welcome. Terms from £4.50 per night.

NORTH YORKSHIRE

CARAVANS FOR HIRE

INGLETON. Mrs Hilary Lund, Lund Holme, Ingleton, Carnforth, Lancashire LA6 3HN (05242 41307). New '93 caravan, sleeps six. Ideal for families. Situated on 200-acre working dairy farm. Visitors are welcome to see the animals or walk through the fields to the river where fishing is available. Facilities include double, twin with third let-down bunk, bathroom with shower, colour TV. Gas and electricity inclusive; pets welcome. We are one mile from Ingleton, famous for caves, waterfalls and Three Peaks. Ideal touring base for Dales, Lakes and Blackpool.

ROBIN HOOD'S BAY. Mrs K.E. Noble, Summerfield Farm, Hawsker, Whitby YO22 4LA (Whitby [0947] 601216). Situated between Whitby and Robin Hood's Bay, one six-berth luxury caravan. All modern conveniences, on secluded private farm site. The grass area is fenced and regularly cut. Safe for children and pets. It is two miles from Whitby and 17 miles from Scarborough, surrounded by 70 acres of arable land. Ten minutes' walk across fields to "Cleveland Way", the footpath leading to the lovely old fishing village of Robin Hood's Bay. Rugged and beautiful coast, sandy beach one mile. Interesting area, riding stables, boating on river, tea gardens, sea fishing, steam railway, zoo, peaceful Esk Valley and moorland villages to visit. Bring hammer and chisel for fossilling. Please provide own linen. Milk on request. Dogs welcome. SAE for details.

SCARBOROUGH. Mr and Mrs P.J. Carter, Roundhills Lodge, Limestone Road, Burniston, Scarborough YO13 0DG (0723 870276). Set in two acres of beautiful countryside with panoramic views of forest and sea. Spacious 6-berth caravan with two fully fitted bedrooms, bathroom with hot and cold water, flush toilet, handbasin and shower. Full size fridge, gas cooker, gas fire, colour TV. Fully equipped except for linen. Three miles from Scarborough and within easy reach of all amenities. Ideal for touring North Yorkshire's lovely countryside. SAE or telephone for details and terms.

SCARBOROUGH.  **Mr and Mrs J.A. Richardson, Carr House Farm, Carr House Lane, Cayton, Scarborough YO11 3ST (0723 376307 or 582341).** From April to end September visitors can enjoy first class accommodation in a six-berth modern caravan on a private and spacious farm site only four miles from the centre of Scarborough. Caravan amenities include electric lighting, fridge, cooker, fire, colour TV, mains toilet and shower room. Private end bedrooms, free gas and electricity. Children welcome. Plenty of room to play, farm animals and horses to see. Excellent base for touring North Yorkshire countryside plus all the attractions of the seaside nearby — beach one and a half miles, sailing, fishing, shows, amusements, etc. Car advisable — village one mile. Terms from £85 to £200 weekly. SAE or phone for vacant dates.

WHITBY near.  **Mrs M. Cana, Partridge Nest Farm, Eskdaleside, Sleights, Whitby YO22 5ES (0947 810450).** Set in the beautiful Esk Valley, six caravans on secluded site in 45 acres of interesting land reaching up to the moors. Just five miles from the sea and the ancient fishing town of Whitby. The North Yorkshire Moors Steam Railway starts two miles away at Grosmont. Ideal for children, bird watchers and all country lovers. Each caravan has mains electric, gas cooker, fire, colour TV, and fridge and all with shower/WC. Ideal touring centre. Riding lessons available on our own horses/ponies. Terms from £85. Phone or write with SAE, please, to **Mrs Cana.**

HOLIDAY PARKS AND CENTRES

HARROGATE. ☼ 💲 𝐀 **Ripley Caravan Park, Ripley, Harrogate HG3 3AU (0423 770050 or 0836 562899).** √ √ √ √ √ Situated adjacent to the delightfully quiet village of Ripley, dominated by its castle which has been occupied by the same family for over 600 years. Conveniently placed for the superb holiday and conference town of Harrogate and for historic Knaresborough; an ideal touring base with the Yorkshire Dales close by. The site facilities include a Leisure Block with games room with colour TV, nursery, playroom, telephone, shop and heated indoor swimming pool, sauna and sun bed; toilet block with showers, ample washbasins, razor points and baby bath. There is a room for our disabled guests with its own specialised facilities. Laundry room, chemical toilet disposal. Electric hook-up points and hard standing for some pitches. Pets welcome. AA Three Pennants. RAC Appointed. Brochure and tariff available on request.

SELBY near. ☼ **Cawood Holiday Park, Ryther Road, Cawood, Near Selby YO8 0TT (0757 268450; Fax: 0757 268537).** There has seldom been a time when a break away in a quiet rural setting has had so much appeal. An opportunity to escape the noise and, often. the pressures of the present age. Here at Cawood Holiday Park, we have worked hard to create an environment which keeps its natural simplicity and at the same time provides a trouble-free holiday. In the last few years we have tried to introduce additional facilities which would be helpful for an elderly or disabled person, and these have now been incorporated, I am sure you will enjoy a stay here; we hope to hear from you soon. Facilities include a licensed bar with a range of bar snacks, occasional cabaret and entertainment, small children's amusement area and pool tables, shop, new shower and toilet block, etc. Brochure available.

Tollerton Park

Situated off A19 between York and Easingwold, Tollerton and Linton-on-Ouse turn-off, Tollerton Park is a select site enjoying panoramic views of Crayke Castle and the White Horse of Kilburn. All mains services are available. For the sport enthusiasts tennis courts are available for daytime use in the village, golf courses at Easingwold and Aldwark, coarse and trout fishing within a mile, and Northallerton Leisure Centre is a 25 minute drive away. Dogs allowed on leads. Season pitches available.

THE STATION INN   A charming country inn is on site offering fine ales and wholesome home cooked food incorporating a beer garden and children's play area.

**Tollerton Park, Tollerton, York, North Yorkshire
Telephone: (0347) 838 313**

CARAVAN SITES AND NIGHT HALTS

EASINGWOLD. 🏕 Å **David and Marjorie Reeder, Hollybrook Touring Park, Pennycarr Lane, Easingwold YO6 3EU (0347 821906).** From York take the A19 to Thirsk, entering Easingwold take right turn at SP Stillington. In quarter-mile turn right into Pennycarr Lane, the site is 700 metres on the right. Delightful small touring park licensed for 30 outfits. Level, grassed, quiet, peaceful and well screened. Modern toilet block with showers, launderette, payphone, Calor gas. Electric hook-ups. Ideally situated for visiting York, North Yorkshire Moors and Dales, Herriot country and East Coast resorts. Pitches from £5.50 per night — concessionary rates for Senior Citizens; no facilities for children. Winter storage available. Dogs welcome, exercised off site, please. Owned by Club members.

HARROGATE. 🏕 Å **Shaw's Trailer Park, Knaresborough Road, Harrogate HG2 7NE (0423 884432).** √ √ √ √ Situated on the A59 between Harrogate and Knaresborough. Bus stop to both towns. Open all year. 24ft entrance, tarmac roads and bays if required. Large playing area for children. Dogs welcome. Sites for caravans (touring), campers, tents. Electrical hook-ups, street lighting, baths, showers, hot water, WCs and chemical disposal. Harrogate — the centre of England, garden city, conference facilities, trade fairs, exhibitions, shows, theatre and fabulous restaurants. Ideal for touring Herriot country, Yorkshire Dales, Harewood House, Fountains Abbey, Bronte country and York. Only minutes to Harrogate and Knaresborough. Please telephone for further details and tariff.

HAWES. 🚐 🏕 Å **Mr and Mrs T.W. Raw, Bainbridge Ings Campsite, Wensleydale, Hawes DL8 3NU (Hawes [0969] 667354).** √ √ √ Three six-berth caravans available on quiet farm with fine views, at head of Wensleydale, one mile east of Hawes, on A684. All well equipped, with gas cooker and fire, electricity and running water. Mains water, flush toilets, hot showers, shaver points, some electric hook-ups and laundry on the site. Children are welcome, and pets allowed if kept on lead. The site is a stone walled meadow. Acreage for 10 motorvans, 40 tents. Country lovers and walkers made very welcome. Wonderful centre for visiting all the Dales. Open April 1st to October 31st. SAE, please, for terms.

KNARESBOROUGH. 🚐 🏕 Å **J.A. and D. Smith, Scotton Park Caravans (Dept. FHG), Scotton, Knaresborough HG5 9HH (0423 864413).** √ √ √ √ √ A quiet, clean, family run park which makes an ideal centre for touring Yorkshire and the Dales. 60 pitches for touring caravans and camping with excellent facilities. There is a children's play area, licensed shop and licensed restaurant; bus stop at entrance. Public telephone on park. Hot and cold water, free hot showers, electric hook-ups. Superb modern five-star caravans and chalets for hire with all mains services, colour TV, no meters. Pets welcome but dogs must be kept on a lead at all times. SAE for brochure.

LEYBURN. 🏕 **The Warden, Lower Wensleydale Caravan Site, Harmby, Leyburn DL8 5PR (0969 23366).**

 From the grassy, quiet, wild-flowered site charmingly laid out in four separate pitching areas you may have the pleasure of exploring Wensleydale. Site is open from the end of March to end of October offering 100 pitches (limited awnings), electric hook-ups. Facilities include WCs, showers, phone, gas. Non-Caravan Club members welcome. Children welcome. Pets welcome if kept on lead. Further details, brochure on request. AAA Caravan Club.

RICHMOND. 🚐 🏕 Å **Mr M.A. Carter, Swaleview Caravan Park, Reeth Road, Richmond DL10 4SF (0748 823106).** Swaleview Caravan Park is situated three miles west of the historic town of Richmond, commonly referred to as "the gateway to the Dales", and is located beside the River Swale in one of the most beautiful areas of the Yorkshire Dales National Park. Facilities include shop, toilets, showers, laundry, telephone, children's play area, games room and fishing. Touring caravans, motor caravans and tents are accepted and hire caravans are available. The Park is ideally situated as a tourist point to explore the Dales and the numerous local attractions. Directions: three miles west of Richmond on A6108; 7 miles A1/A1(M). SAE, please, for brochure. Open March to October. ETB and Humberside and Yorks TB registered. Terms: car and caravan £5.30 per night.

RICHMOND. ⬛ 🄰 **Brompton-on-Swale Caravan Park, Richmond DL10 7EZ (0748 824629).** √ √ √ √ Explore the Yorkshire Dales and relax in lovely natural surroundings on the banks of the River Swale which provides fishing and scenic walks. Caravans, tents and motorhomes all welcome. The two new toilet and shower blocks have hot water, hair dryers, shaver sockets, facilities for disabled visitors, a laundry with washers, dryers and iron. This family-run park offers electricity points, holiday flats with colour TV, a well stocked shop, children's play area and TV room. Short grass. Dogs welcome, on a lead. Exit A1 at Catterick A6136, follow B6271 through Brompton-on-Swale to Richmond, park on left 1½ miles south east of Richmond.

RIPON. ⬛ **Ure Bank Caravan Park, Ure Bank, Ripon (0765 602964).** √ √ √ √ Situated approximately four miles from the A1. Surrounded by the rolling green fields of North Yorkshire, this beautifully located park is just a few minutes' walk from the historic town centre and ancient Cathedral of Ripon. Ideally placed at the gateway to the North Yorkshire Dales, the site serves as a superb base to explore the scenic countryside on its doorstep; also easy access to Lake District. Site facilities include showers, toilets and laundry blocks with hot and cold water, automatic washing machines available; self-service shop including off-licence; lounge bar, games room; bar meals. Swimming and boating on river, fishing licences available; swings, slides etc for children. Seasonal touring pitches available. Open 1st March to 31st October. Car parking. Dogs allowed on lead. Brochure.

SCARBOROUGH. ⬛ 🄰 **Mrs Carol Croft, Cayton Village Caravan Park (Dept 5), Mill Lane, Cayton Bay, Scarborough YO11 3NN (0723 583171 or 0904 624630).** Family-run park. Spacious, sheltered landscaped park for 160 tourers, tents or motor homes, situated half a mile from beach, three miles from Scarborough, four miles from Filey. Adjoining Cayton village church; two pubs, fish and chip shop, post office and bus service within 150 yards. The park has free showers and washing up facilities. Children's adventure playground where caravans and tents can be placed in view of the playground. Laundry, shop with Calor and Camping Gaz, electric hook-ups to tents and caravans, chemical toilet disposal. A three-acre dog walk. Seasonal pitches are available from Easter to October 1st. Please send for brochure.

SPRING WILLOWS

TOURING CARAVAN AND CAMPING PARK

AA ▶▶

RAC

The Gateway to the Yorkshire Coast... This superb family holiday park has been beautifully landscaped around a springwater stream, winding through the beergarden and broadwalk, surrounded by sanddunes creating a magnificent suntrap protecting you from coastal winds.
Our family friendly facilities reflect what you expect from a perfect touring holiday.
Free modern heated pool, *indoor play complex, large adventure playground, luxurious heated toilet and showerrooms including* **disabled facilities.**
Club with good atmosphere, **conservatory,** *barmeals, shop, take-away,* **sauna, solarium,** *launderette. We also cater for rallies and remain open for* **wintertouring.** *Sounds good... it is!*

For more information, please send a s.a.e. to
Spring Willows Touring Park, Main Road, Staxton, Nr. Scarborough, YO12 4SB or ring 0723 891505

SCARBOROUGH (Cayton Bay). ⬛ **Mr and Mrs R.J. and D. Brown, Brown's Caravan Park, Mill Lane, Cayton Bay YO11 3NN (Scarborough [0723] 582303).** From Scarborough take A165 south for three miles. Turn right at Cayton Bay traffic lights, site after 200 yards on right. Signposted. Quiet family park, grassy and level. Ten minutes' walk from beach or village local. Launderette, Games room. Extra charge for caravan awnings and electric hook-ups. Open April to September. Ideal touring centre for North Yorkshire; situated mid-way between Scarborough and Filey. There are 110 privately owned static holiday caravans; 35 tourers. Terms from £6.00. Enquiries welcome.

WHITBY. ⬛ 🄰 **D.I. Jackson, York House Caravan Park, Hawsker, Whitby YO22 4LW (0947 880354).** Situated on the North Yorkshire coast in the National Park, with panoramic views over the North Sea, Yorkshire Moors and Whitby. Grass site, mainly level, with access roads and clearly defined pitches. Well screened with trees and hedges. Amenities include modern toilet block with showers, sinks, toilets, hot water, washer and spin dryer, and washing-up sinks. Some electric hook-ups. Shop. Children and pets welcome. Rates from £4 to £6.50 per night. Reductions for whole weeks. Open March to October inclusive. AA 3 Pennants.

NORTH YORKSHIRE – RICH IN TOURIST ATTRACTIONS!

Dales, moors, castles, abbeys, cathedrals – you name it and you're almost sure to find it in North Yorkshire. Leading attractions include Castle Howard, the moorlands walks at Goathland, the Waterfalls at Falling Foss, Skipton, Richmond, Wensleydale, Bridestones Moor, Ripon Cathedral, Whitby, Settle and, of course, York itself.

YORK. 🔲 🛆 **"Riverside" Caravan & Camping Park, Ferry Lane, Bishopthorpe, York YO2 1SB**

(0904 704442 or 0904 705812). A small secluded site located on the edge of the River Ouse at Bishopthorpe, two miles south of York near Bishopthorpe Palace, the home of the Archbishop of York. Just 25 pitches, five of which are for caravans, on a flat site with many trees around and riverside walks to Acaster Malbis and York. Numerous facilities include riverbus service into York daily, restaurant with barbecues, boat slipway, fishing, children's play area, boat hire, picnic tables and electric hook-ups, etc. Modern toilets and showers with hairdryers, shaver sockets, and utility room with fridge, spin dryer, large sinks and constant hot water. A friendly site with lots to offer. Brochure available.

YORK. 🔲 🛆 **J.C. Scutt, Swallow Hall, Crockey Hill, York YO1 4SG (0904 448219).** Secluded sheltered site on a small farm surrounded by Forestry Commission woodland walks. Historic York, Viking centre, Railway Museum, Air Museum six minutes' drive. New 18-hole Par 3 golf course, tennis, fishing, riding, two nature reserves close by. Clay pigeon shooting by arrangement. North Yorks Moors 30 minutes. Touring caravans, tents and motor homes welcome. Open 1st March to 31st October. Facilities include: hot showers, flush toilets, shaver points and chemical disposal point. Gas bottles. Dogs accepted. Children's play area, golf. Terms on application.

CAMPING SITES

SCARBOROUGH. 🔲 🛆 **Mrs Carol Croft, Cayton Village Caravan Park (Dept 5), Mill Lane, Cayton Bay, Scarborough YO11 3NN (0723 583171 or 0904 624630).** Family-run park. Spacious, sheltered landscaped park for 160 tourers, tents or motor homes, situated half a mile from beach, three miles from Scarborough, four miles from Filey. Adjoining Cayton village church; two pubs, fish and chip shop, post office and bus service within 150 yards. The park has free showers and washing up facilities. Children's adventure playground where caravans and tents can be placed in view of the playground. Laundry, shop with Calor and Camping Gaz, electric hook-ups to tents and caravans, chemical toilet disposal. A three-acre dog walk. Seasonal pitches are available from Easter to October 1st. Please send for brochure.

WEST YORKSHIRE

CARAVANS FOR HIRE

HOLMFIRTH. 🚐 🔲 🛆 **Holme Valley Camping and Caravan Park, Thongsbridge, Holmfirth**

HD7 2TD (0484 665819). √ √ √ √ In picturesque valley-bottom location in the heart of "Summer Wine" country on fringe of Peak District National Park, we are one mile north of Holmfirth off A6024. Our clean, modern amenities include first-rate toilet and shower block, launderette, washing-up area, chemical toilet disposal unit; also well stocked licensed shop, hot take-aways at peak periods, kiddies' play area, solarium and on-site angling in both river and small lake. We have a total of 58 level touring pitches from £5 per night, electric hook-ups to all and tourer-type hire caravans (two/five berth) from £75 per week. Brochure available free from: **Mr and Mrs P.M. Peaker.**

PLEASE ENCLOSE A STAMPED ADDRESSED
ENVELOPE WITH ENQUIRIES

CARAVAN SITES AND NIGHT HALTS

HAWORTH near.  **Upwood Holiday Park, Blackmoor Road, Oxenhope, Near Haworth, Keighley BD22 9SS (Haworth [0535] 643254).** Attractive country site on small farm enjoying peaceful surroundings and panoramic views, situated one mile from the Bronte village of Haworth, with good walks and riding close by. Close to the beautiful Yorkshire Dales and many places of historical interest, yet within easy reach of a host of bargain mill shops. Well-kept level site with modern toilets and showers and electrical hook-ups. Games rooms with table tennis and pool, bar adjacent with family room serving good selection of bar meals. Launderette and ironing facilities. Fully serviced luxury holiday caravans with colour TV to let at reasonable rates, each completely equipped including bed linen. SAE to **D. & M. Wasley.**

HOLMFIRTH.  **Holme Valley Camping and Caravan Park, Thongsbridge, Holmfirth HD7 2TD (0484 665819).** √ √ √ √ In picturesque valley-bottom location in the heart of "Summer Wine" country on fringe of Peak District National Park, we are one mile north of Holmfirth off A6024. Our clean, modern amenities include first-rate toilet and shower block, launderette, washing-up area, chemical toilet disposal unit; also well stocked licensed shop, hot take-aways at peak periods, kiddies' play area, solarium and on-site angling in both river and small lake. We have a total of 58 level touring pitches from £5 per night, electric hook-ups to all and tourer-type hire caravans (two/five berth) from £75 per week. Brochure available free from: **Mr and Mrs P.M. Peaker.**

CAMPING SITES

HOLMFIRTH.  **Holme Valley Camping and Caravan Park, Thongsbridge, Holmfirth HD7 2TD (0484 665819).** √ √ √ √ In picturesque valley-bottom location in the heart of "Summer Wine" country on fringe of Peak District National Park, we are one mile north of Holmfirth off A6024. Our clean, modern amenities include first-rate toilet and shower block, launderette, washing-up area, chemical toilet disposal unit; also well stocked licensed shop, hot take-aways at peak periods, kiddies' play area, solarium and on-site angling in both river and small lake. We have a total of 58 level touring pitches from £5 per night, electric hook-ups to all and tourer-type hire caravans (two/five berth) from £75 per week. Brochure available free from: **Mr and Mrs P.M. Peaker.**

FHG DIPLOMA WINNERS 1993

Each year we award a small number of diplomas to holiday proprietors whose services have been specially commended by our readers and the following advertisers were our FHG Diploma winners for 1993.

ENGLAND

John & Diane Parry, White Lodge Hotel, Near Newquay, Cornwall
Alan & Linda Bleasdale, Borwick Lodge, Hawkshead, Ambleside, Cumbria
Mrs Mary Hollingsworth, Collycroft Farm, Near Ashbourne, Derbyshire
Mrs D.A. Douse, Spicers Farm, Braintree, Essex
Mr & Mrs F.J. Matthews, The Hayes, Corbridge, Northumberland
Mr R.H. Miles & Mr P.J. Harrison, The Beckford Arms, Fonthill Gifford, Wiltshire
Mr & Mrs R.S. Burke, Friar Lodge, Saddleworth, West Yorkshire

SCOTLAND

Mr & Mrs A.G. Ward, Glen Loy Lodge, Near Fort William, Inverness-shire
Mr & Mrs R.I. Campbell, Pitnacree Cottage Guest House, Ballinluig, Perthshire

WALES

D. & J. Canton, Nolton Haven Farm, Nolton Haven, Dyfed

ISLE OF MAN

CAMPING SITES

MAUGHOLD. ⚕ Lewaigue Farm Camp, Maughold. Explore the Island from bunkhouse facility in purpose converted farm, close to sea. Full self-catering. Sleeps a maximum of 60. Hot showers, camp fire, big games room. Great for youth groups, cycle/diving clubs, etc. Rates from £3.95 per person per night. Open all season. Colour brochure available on request **(0624 812216 24 hours).**

ISLE OF WIGHT

CARAVANS FOR HIRE

THORNESS BAY. 🚐 **Pat Berrow, 47 Albert Street, Cowes PO31 7ND (0983 298319).** Eight berth luxury caravan on Haven/Warner site in a woodland setting. Full facilities including pools, shop, restaurant/bars. Entertainment/games, for adults, teenagers and children. Access to beach and coastal path. Short drives to numerous local attractions and beauty spots. Horse riding on site. Pets welcome. Haven/Warner facilities at discounted prices £170 to £410 per week according to season (colour TV, gas, hot water, electricity inclusive). Brochure available.

HOLIDAY PARKS AND CENTRES

TOTLAND BAY. ☼ **Heathfield Farm Campsite, Mrs F.G. Osman, Ivylands Holiday Park, The Broadway, Totland Bay PO39 0AN (0983 752480).**

√ √ √ √ √ Family camping for tents, tourers and motor caravans on level grass site. Attractive rural area with delightful downland and sea views. Amenities include modern toilet block with free hot showers, flush toilets, shaver points, hairdryers, dishwashing area, waste disposal point and use of launderette at nearby Ivylands Holiday Park. Within easy walking distance of shops, buses, pubs, safe sandy beaches and local indoor swimming pool. Located just off the A3054 Yarmouth to Totland Road 5 minutes from Yarmouth ferry port.

CARAVAN SITES AND NIGHT HALTS

CAMPING SITES

SCOTLAND

ANGUS

CARAVAN SITES AND NIGHT HALTS

MONTROSE. 🚐 💲 ⛺ **Littlewood Park, Brechin Road, Montrose DD10 9LE (0674 72973).**

√ √ √ √ Lovely little park with beautiful views over Montrose Basin Bird Reserve. Close to shops, pool and beach. Letting units include new six-person pine cottage with every luxury including double glazing and full heating, situated in prime viewing spot over bird reserve. From £200 per week. We also have new or recent model Thistle Award Holiday Homes, with colour TVs, videos, microwaves, toasters and all bedding. From £115 per week. Area for tourers with electric hook-ups, toilets, showers and laundry. Constant free hot water. Personally supervised by **Margaret and John Kelly** who guarantee a friendly welcome.

ARGYLL

CARAVAN SITES AND NIGHT HALTS

GLENDARUEL. 🚐 💲 ⛺ **Glendaruel Caravan and Camping Park (FHG), Glendaruel PA22 3AB**

(Tel & Fax: 036-982 267). √ √ √ √ √ Unwind and relax in the peaceful atmosphere of this beautiful award-winning country park, personally run by the owners Quin and Anne Craig. Discover an area of outstanding natural beauty, hidden sandy beaches, great walking, bird watching, golf and fishing. Kyles of Bute and sea sports five miles. Bicycle hire. Thistle Award caravan holiday homes for hire, all-weather touring pitches with electric hook-ups. Reduced Clyde ferry fares and various local discounts. Please send for our colour brochure.

STRATHCLYDE REGION – WHERE TO START?

Scotland's most densely populated region houses more people than many small countries. At its centre is Glasgow where you will find many attractions including the Art Gallery and the Burrell Collection. Heading further out this Region includes such popular places as Oban, the Mull of Kintyre, the Clyde Valley, the Ayrshire Coast and Argyll Forest Park.

APPIN HOLIDAY CARAVANS

The Scottish Highlands and Islands

Truly magnificent setting right on the Lochside

8 very private caravans. All recent models, each fully serviced.
Laundrette, recreation room, play area and babysitting.
FREE fishing (salt and freshwater). Boating and sailing, great hill walks.
Pony trekking and Licensed Inn nearby.
Special Spring and Autumn terms. Price Guide – £135 to £235 per unit weekly.

Please send SAE for colour brochure giving dates required.

**Mr & Mrs I. Weir, Appin Holiday Caravans, Appin,
Argyll PA38 4BQ   Telephone: Appin 287 (063173-287)**

FHG
DIPLOMA
WINNER

For more details, see our advert in the colour section of this guide.

ISLE OF COLL (Inner Hebrides). 🅢 Å **Mrs P. Graham, Garden House, Isle of Coll PA78 6TB (087 93374).**

This is a natural history Paradise with unspoilt beaches and views of the West Coast and islands. Peace and quiet with no crowds. We are on the south-west of the island, four miles from the village and pier, next door to RSPB Nature Reserve. The flat, grassy site is sheltered, has running water, a toilet and chemical disposal point. There is a picnic area and facilities for barbecue/camp fire. A small working farm provides vegetables (in season), also eggs. Children and pets by arrangement. Terms for visitors, £2.00 per person per night. Ferries leave Oban for Coll and Tiree, foot passengers can join at Tobermory, Mull. Write or phone for details.

KINLOCHLEVEN. 🚐 🅢 Å **Mr and Mrs Colin Cameron, Caolasnacon Caravan and Camping Park, Kinlochleven PA40 4RS (Kinlochleven [085-54] 279).**

There are 20 static six-berth caravans for holiday hire on this lovely site with breathtaking mountain scenery on edge of Loch Leven. They have electric lighting, Calor gas cookers and heaters, toilet, shower, fridge and colour TV. An ideal touring centre. There are two toilet blocks with hot water and showers and laundry facilities. Children are welcome and pets allowed. Open from April to October. Milk, gas, soft drinks available on site; shops three miles. There is sea-loch fishing, hill walking and boating. Boats and rods for hire, fishing tackle for sale. Weekly rates for hiring vans from £120 to £220, with 5% reductions on two-week bookings. For tourers from £5.75 nightly. There are seven and a half acres for campers and rates are from £3.50 nightly.

OBAN. ▣ ▣ ⋀ **Brian and Sylvia Thompson, Oban Caravan and Camping Park, Gallanach-more Farm, Oban PA34 (0631 62425).** ✓ ✓ ✓ ✓ In an area of outstanding scenic beauty and graded as "Very Good", Gallanachmore Farm is situated on the seafront overlooking the Island of Kerrera. The Park provides excellent toilet and shower facilities, a well-stocked shop, launderette, children's play area and lends itself superbly for boating, fishing, windsurfing and scuba diving holidays. Situated two and a half miles south of Oban; from roundabout in the centre of the town, follow signs to Gallanach.

AYRSHIRE

CARAVANS FOR HIRE

AYR near. ▣ ▣ ⋀ **Middlemuir Park, Tarbolton, Near Ayr KA5 5NR (0292 541647; Fax: 0292 541649).** ✓ ✓ ✓ ✓ In the very heart of Burns Country. Quiet, family-run Holiday Park situated in the old walled gardens of the Castle O'Montgomerie, five miles east of Ayr on the B743. A golfers' paradise — 18 courses within very easy reach. The sport of kings — Ayr Racecourse approximately seven miles. New luxury caravans to let with all services, also a full complement of equipment, including supplementary heating. Top of the range caravans are provided with bed linen, towels, microwaves, hair dryers, clock radios, etc. Children's play area, games room, launderette and pay phone. Pets welcome, dog walk provided. Touring caravan pitches, all with electric hook-up. STB Thistle Award. RAC Appointed. The Site where "Excellence" comes as Standard.

IRVINE. ▣ ▣ ⋀ **Mr John Sim, Cunninghamhead Estate Caravan Park, Irvine, Kilmarnock KA3 2PE (029 485 0238).** Beautiful country park only three and a half miles from Irvine's town centre shopping. You can visit Scotland's number one attraction, "The Magnum Leisure Centre". Enjoy a sail on the Clyde, play golf on one of the many courses, or relax at the Beach Park. Lots of variety — all nearby. Modern four/six/eight-berth caravans for hire. Tourers, tents, caravanettes welcome. Laundry, toilets, showers, chemical disposal, play area and bar with games room. Easy travel to Glasgow, Ayr, Troon, and the Ardrossan/Arran ferry. From Irvine take A736 to Stanecastle roundabout, then B769 Stewarton Road for two and a half miles. Caravan Park on left. From £85 to £220 weekly. Brochure.

CARAVAN SITES AND NIGHT HALTS

MAIDENS. ▣ **Sandy Beach Caravan Park, Ardlochan Road, Maidens KA26 9NS (0655 31456).** Proprietor: Derek Braid. The Park offers six touring pitches, each with electric hook-up. There is a toilet block with coin-operated showers and coin-operated laundry with tumble dryer. There is a shop/general store and snack/coffee shop at site entrance. Children and pets welcome. Just 50 yards from safe, sandy beach and an ideal base for touring Burns' country. A mile from Culzean Castle, Scotland's most visited country park. Turnberry Golf Course, venue for the 1994 British Open, is just a mile away, and there are 15 other courses within 45 minutes of Maidens. Terms from £8.50 per night; one third deposit required on booking, with the balance payable on arrival. To find us, turn off A77 signposted Turnberry/Maidens; Maidens is approximately two miles.

CAITHNESS

CARAVAN SITES AND NIGHT HALTS

JOHN O'GROATS. 🏕 Å **John O'Groats Caravan and Camping Site, John O'Groats KW1 4YS (095581 329).** √ √ √ 3 Pennants. At end of A9 on seafront beside "last house in Scotland", caravan and camping site with showers, launderette and disabled toilet. Caravans, caravanettes and tents welcome. Booking office for day trips to Orkney Islands on site. Hotel, restaurant, café, harbour 150 metres. Magnificent cliff scenery with sea birds galore including puffins, guillemots, skuas within one and a half miles. Seals are often seen swimming to and fro and there is a seal colony only four miles away. From the site you can see the wide panorama of the Orkney Islands, the nearest of which is only seven miles away. Prices from £5 per night. Public telephone on site.

THURSO. 📺 🏕 Å **Thurso Caravan and Camping Site, Thurso.** √ √ √ √ A lovely four and a half acre site overlooking Thurso Bay, with view of Orkney Islands in background. Open May to September. 80 touring pitches, 50 camping sites and many facilities include showers, shaver points, launderette with drying/ironing. Electric hook-ups, car park, telephone. Dogs welcome. Sports available locally include loch and sea fishing (boat and beach), surfing, sea canoeing, sub-aqua diving, yachting, pony trekking, golf, coastal walks, sea bird colonies. Pay for six nights and get a seventh night free! Further details and terms available on request from: **Mr Holmes, Caithness District Council, Council Offices, Wick KW1 4AB (0955 3761).**

CLACKMANNANSHIRE

CARAVAN SITES AND NIGHT HALTS

DOLLAR. 🏕 Å **Mrs A. Small, Riverside Caravan Park, Dollar FK14 7LX (0259 742896).** √ √ √ Site of seven acres — 30 statics (not for hire), 30 touring vans/tents. Grassy, level pitches on riverbank. Situation on B913, half-mile south of Dollar, which is an attractive hillfoot town with steeply wooded glen dominated by Castle Campbell. Ideal for anglers and hillwalkers, and a central base from which to tour the area. Site facilities include toilets, showers, shop, Calor gas sales, electric hook-up points. Free fishing on site; golf, swimming, riding all available nearby. Pets welcome. Open 1st April – 6th October. Tourist Board registered.

DUMFRIESSHIRE

CARAVANS FOR HIRE

SOUTHERNESS. 📺 🏕 Å **Mr and Mrs J.A. Robertson, Lighthouse Leisure, Southerness DG2 8AZ (038788 277).** √ √ √

Quiet, lawned family park situated by unspoilt sweeping sandy beaches, 15 miles south of Dumfries. Next to all village facilities, pubs, entertainment, children's Toytown. Excellent fishing — sea and freshwater — in the vicinity. Pony trekking nearby. Overlooking 18-hole championship golf course, with five others in a 16-mile radius. Luxury new and nearly new caravans for hire. All with baths and showers, serviced, with gas and electricity. Fully equipped except for linen. Mountain bikes for hire. Launderette, playpark and modern shower block. Grass pitches with electric hook-ups for touring caravans and tents. Tourist Board registered. Colour brochures on request.

CARAVAN SITES AND NIGHT HALTS

ECCLEFECHAN. 🚐 💲 🏕 **Cressfield Caravan Park, Ecclefechan, Near Lockerbie DG11 3RD (0576 300702).** √ √ √ √ √ This is a peaceful, well-kept park set in beautiful, undulating countryside quarter of a mile from A/M74, 10 miles north of Gretna. A convenient stopover on the North/South route, and an excellent base for walking, cycling, fishing, golf, birdwatching and touring in South West Scotland, the Borders, Northumberland and Cumbria. OPEN ALL YEAR. Superb facilities: heated laundry/toilets, free showers, bath in ladies', individual cubicles, facilities for the disabled. Hard standing and electric hook-ups for all touring pitches. Grass area for tents. Motorhomes and rallies welcome (10-30 units). Children's play area, dog exercise area, payphone, golf nets; hotel adjacent, village amenities close by. Static pitches and luxury holiday homes to let, on one of Scotland's top ten parks (Practical Caravan '93). Telephone for a FREE Brochure.

EDINBURGH & THE LOTHIANS

CARAVANS FOR HIRE

🚐 Caravans for Hire (one or more caravans for hire on a site)

☼ Holiday Parks & Centres (usually larger sites hiring holiday homes/vans, with amenities)

💲 Caravan Sites (for touring caravans, caravanettes, etc.)

🏕 Camping Sites (where campers are welcome)

CARAVAN SITES AND NIGHT HALTS

EDINBURGH. 💲 **Little France Caravan Park, Old Dalkeith Road, Edinburgh (031-666 2326).** √ √ √ √ Situated on the A7 south of the city. Direct access to city centre (three miles) by car or public transport. All of Edinburgh's amenities easily accessible from the caravan site — Royal Commonwealth Pool, Museum, Castle, Botanic Gardens, Royal Mile, theatres, cinemas, Meadowbank Sports Centre. On site facilities include a laundry room and electric hook-ups. Opposite the park there is a lounge bar which provides bar lunches. Further information on request.

HADDINGTON. 🛏 💲 Å **The Monks' Muir, Haddington EH41 3SB (Tel and Fax: 0620 860340).**

√ √ √ √ A delightfully secluded, friendly, green, sheltered place, but with direct access to the main A1 road. One of the oldest and best-loved caravan and camping parks in Scotland, cherished by its owners and full of birdsong. Only 25 minutes from Edinburgh, in an area of great beauty with glorious beaches, rich farmland, a plethora of golf courses and fascinating villages. Excellent facilities including the best park shop and café/bistro in the business! Appointed by every motoring and caravanning organisation, and with the Scottish Tourist Board "Thistle" Award for excellence. Lovely pitches for tourers, tents or campervans — or hire our luxury six/eight berth holiday homes, totally equipped and thoughtfully presented. Discounted golf tickets, off-season midweek and weekend breaks, price reductions for over 55's and open all year round!

NORTH BERWICK. 🛏 💲 **Mr and Mrs W.R. Macnair, Gilsland Caravan Park, Grange Road, North Berwick EH39 5JA (North Berwick [0620] 2205).** Situated one mile from seaside resort of North Berwick, famous for golf and popular with families who prefer a quiet holiday. We are 24 miles from Edinburgh, within easy reach of the Border Country and a good centre for touring. Gilsland is a clean, well kept site of 150 holiday vans. We offer, on site, flush toilets, showers and hot water. A list of tenants who let their vans can be obtained — send SAE please. We have 30 touring stances at £9 per night. No advance booking.

FIFE

CARAVAN SITES AND NIGHT HALTS

KIRKCALDY. 💲 Å **Dunnikier Caravan Park, Dunnikier Way, Kirkcaldy KY1 3ND (0592 267563).** BH&HPA, RAC, AA. A beautiful country caravan park on level ground situated within Dunnikier Estate. Golf course and Hotel are only eight minutes' walk from the site. Easy commuting distance between Edinburgh, Dundee, Aberdeen; within easy reach of all Fife's golf courses. The Park has 60 pitches, 32 with electric points, and can accommodate touring caravans, motor homes and tents. We can boast excellent facilities — showers, washbasins, toilets, separate invalid toilet with own shower, chemical disposal, laundry and outside dishwashing for campers. There is a convenience store on site and a supermarket located 500 yards away. Caravans from £7 per night, tents from £5; stay seven consecutive nights, get one night free.

INVERNESS-SHIRE

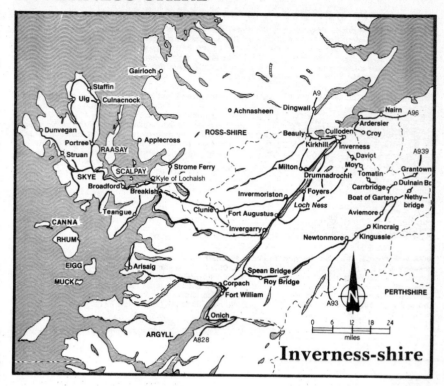

Inverness-shire

CARAVANS FOR HIRE

FORT WILLIAM.  **Mr J. Fraser, Cross Cottage, 20 N. Ballachulish, Onich, Fort William PH33 6RZ (Onich [08553] 335).** Set among panorama of mountain and loch, this small site has eight modern caravans to offer. It is especially attractive to visitors who prefer a peaceful, informal holiday away from the crowds. Personal attention guaranteed. Each unit — large six-berths (25 ft to 34 ft) — has toilet, electric fridge, gas fire and cooker, colour TV, power point; shower, hot and cold, plus washbasin. Site amenities include laundry facilities and play area for children and their pets. Boats for hire. Beach 200 yards. Post office, shops within two miles. Area is ideal for hill-walking, forest trails, fishing etc. and abounds in places of interest — Glencoe, Bonnie Prince Charlie Country and the romantic Islands. Open all year. Terms from £135 to £270. Tourist Board registered.

SPEAN BRIDGE. **Mrs M. H. Cairns, Invergloy House, Spean Bridge PH34 4DY (0397 712681). Sleeps 5.** Two luxury caravans to let, one 29' (double bedroom, double berth and one single berth), and the other 31' (double bedroom, twin/double second bedroom, single berth). Each sleeps five. Fully equipped except linen. Shower, toilet, washbasin; Calor gas heating and cooking, electric fridge and lighting. Situated in beautiful secluded grounds overlooking Loch Lochy (50 acres), beach reached by foot-path. Free fishing, rowing boats for hire and hard tennis court. Supermarket five miles away in Spean Bridge. Pony trekking and golf nearby. Skye, Inverness, Aviemore and Western Highlands easily reached. Children welcome. Controlled dog welcome. Open April 1st to October 31st. Weekly terms from £160 to £220. (Daily letting out of high season; £10 discount for two week booking for over two occupancy). SAE please, for further details. Early and late months are particularly attractive for a holiday in peaceful surroundings. Tourist Board registered.

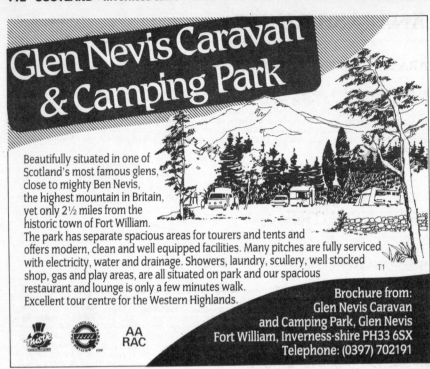

Glen Nevis Caravan & Camping Park

Beautifully situated in one of Scotland's most famous glens, close to mighty Ben Nevis, the highest mountain in Britain, yet only 2½ miles from the historic town of Fort William. The park has separate spacious areas for tourers and tents and offers modern, clean and well equipped facilities. Many pitches are fully serviced with electricity, water and drainage. Showers, laundry, scullery, well stocked shop, gas and play areas, are all situated on park and our spacious restaurant and lounge is only a few minutes walk. Excellent tour centre for the Western Highlands.

T1

Brochure from:
Glen Nevis Caravan and Camping Park, Glen Nevis
Fort William, Inverness-shire PH33 6SX
Telephone: (0397) 702191

AA
RAC

CARAVAN SITES AND NIGHT HALTS

FORRES by. 🅂 Å **Findhorn Sands Caravan Park, By Forres, Morayshire IV36 0YZ (Findhorn [0309] 690324).** √ √ √ √ On this Caravan Park there are 45 touring pitches for Caravans, Caravanettes and Tents. The site has shops and bars nearby. Sporting facilities include water ski-ing, yachting and safe bathing. Write or phone for rates and full details. Book for seven nights — one free. Access to site via Dunes Road.

INVERNESS. 🚐 Å **Bunchrew Caravan Park, Bunchrew, Inverness IV3 6TD (0463 237802).**

√ √ √ √ Surrounded by mature woodland and set in 20 acres of peaceful parkland overlooking the Beauly Firth, situated just three miles west of Inverness on the A862 Beauly Road. A wonderful holiday base for touring the Highlands, with excellent sporting and leisure facilities set in and around Inverness. Level, sheltered, grassy pitches for tents and tourers, with 50 electric hook-up points. Other facilities include free showers, children's play areas, well-stocked park shop, telephone, launderette and dishwashing area. Calor gas available on site. Thistle Award-winning fully equipped luxury caravan holiday homes for hire. Open 15 March to 15 October. ANWB Recommended.

NAIRN. 🅂 Å **Spindrift Caravan & Camping Park, Little Kildrummie, Nairn IV12 5QU (0667 53992).** √ √ √ √ √ This small, secluded park, sheltered by trees and overlooking the River Nairn and distant Monadlaith Mountains is an ideal base from which to explore Morayshire's wealth of history. The popular holiday resort of Nairn, with its lovely sandy beaches, is just one and a half miles away. Fishing is available (permits from reception) and Nairn itself has two 18-hole golf courses. There is also a heated swimming pool, squash or tennis courts and many fine restaurants and shops just five minutes away by car. The park has modern toilet blocks with free showers. Launderette, chemical disposal points and electric hook-ups. Pets are welcome. For details contact **Bernard J. Guillot.**

LANARKSHIRE

CARAVAN SITES AND NIGHT HALTS

KIRKFIELDBANK. 💲 🏕 **Mr Jim McWhinnie, Clyde Valley Caravan Park, Kirkfieldbank, Lanark (Lanark [0555] 66 3951 or [0698] 357 684).** Situated in the beautiful Clyde Valley, with two excellent fishing rivers running by, this 10-acre site offers facilities for up to 50 touring caravans. Amenities include sanitation, water supply, electricity hook-up, showers, laundry. Shops, golf, pony trekking nearby. Children welcome; pets welcome. Rates for caravans £5.00 per night; also two acres for campers — £5.00 per night. Electric hook-up £1.50 per night, Awning £1.00 per night. Open 1st April to end October. Tourist Board registered.

PEEBLESSHIRE

CARAVAN SITES AND NIGHT HALTS

PEEBLES. 🚐 💲 🏕 **Rosetta Caravan and Camping Park, Rosetta Road, Peebles EH45 8PG (0721 720770).** √ √ √ √ √ In the beautiful Scottish Border country, static caravans to let, fully equipped with every modern convenience. We also have facilities for touring caravans and campers; toilet block and washing/laundry rooms; on-site shop; play area; licensed bar; putting and bowling greens. A wonderful area for walking, riding, golf and fishing on the River Tweed. Central for touring — Edinburgh only a short drive away. Brochure available. AA 3 Pennants; RAC Approved.

PERTHSHIRE

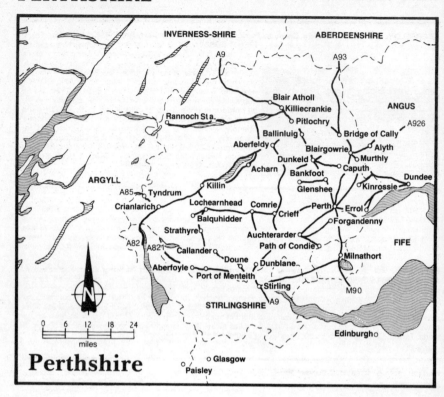

Perthshire

CARAVANS FOR HIRE

Terms quoted in this publication may be subject to increase if rises in costs necessitate

CARAVAN SITES AND NIGHT HALTS

ABERFELDY. 🏕 ⛺ **Aberfeldy Caravan Park, Dunkeld Road, Aberfeldy PH15 2AQ (Aberfeldy**

[0887] 20662). √ √ √ √ AA 3 Pennants. Managed by the Leisure and Recreation Department of Perth and Kinross District Council, the park recently underwent upgrading. Ideally situated on the banks of the River Tay, the park is well placed for day trips and touring. Oban, Fort William, Inverness, the Trossachs, Perth and even the East Coast are all accessible via spectacular roads. There are opportunities for all outdoor activities — golf, hillwalking, fishing, sailing and water sports in an area rich in wildlife and rugged splendour. Friendly service and high standards. Sports discount for seven-day stays and off-peak Senior Citizen discounts. Caravans from £5.80 per night. Tents from £4 per night. RAC and Caravan Club Listed. Free brochure from **3 High Street, Perth (0738 39911 ext. 3602).**

COMRIE (near Crieff). 🚐 🏕 ⛺ **P.J. & E.L. Gill, West Lodge Caravan Park, Comrie PH6 2LS (0764 670354).** √ √ √ Pleasant family-run caravan and camping park. Good touring area. Excellent facilities on the park including flush toilets, hot showers, laundry area, shop, gas and telephone. Pitches have electric hook-ups. Six six-berth static vans for hire, all with toilets and running water; some with showers. Children and pets welcome. Caravans from £5; Tents from £4. Prior booking required July and August. Ring for information — brochure sent on request.

KENMORE. 🏕 ⛺ **Kenmore Caravan and Camping Park, Taymouth Holiday Centre, Kenmore, Aberfeldy PH15 2HN (0887 830226).** √ √ √ Pleasant site by the River Tay. Ideal touring centre, beautiful forest and hill walks in the vicinity, or mountain treks up Ben Lawers or Schiehallion. Excellent new golf course (par 70) on site, with others nearby. Fishing on the river or Loch Tay. Most water activities, pony trekking available. Site offers a recreation field, two children's play areas, a dog-walking area; hook-up points plus all necessary amenities. Bar food can be bought in our own Byre Bistro, and there are many local eating places as well. Swimming pool at Aberfeldy, six miles away. Quiet site at night, owner supervised. Dogs on leads. Terms: Caravans from £6.50, tents from £5.50. AA/RAC four Pennants.

PERTH. 🏕 ⛺ **Cleeve Caravan Park, Glasgow Road, Perth PH2 0PH (Perth [0738] 39521).**

√ √ √ √ √ AA 3 Pennant. Perth is a beautiful city situated on a scenic stretch of the River Tay. Cleeve Caravan Park is on the western outskirts, five minutes from central Perth, in a quiet woodland setting. The park is renowned for its friendly service and high standards. Managed by Perth and Kinross District Council Leisure and Recreation Department, Cleeve is ideally situated for visits to coast, glen, mountain and loch. In Perth itself there is much activity, good eating out and the best leisure pool in Scotland. 80 pitches. Booking available. Sports facility discount for seven-day stays off-season and Senior Citizen off-peak discounts. Caravans from £5.80 per night. Tents from £4 per night. RAC and Caravan Club Listed. Free brochure from **3 High Street, Perth (0738 39911 ext. 3602).**

ROSS-SHIRE

CARAVANS FOR HIRE

POOLEWE. 🚐 **Mrs A.E. Ella, "Sonas", Cove, Poolewe IV22 2LT (044 586 203).** Four strategically placed six-berth caravans and croft house sleeping eight are situated in a crofting hamlet on the shore of Loch Ewe. All have an uninterrupted panoramic view of sea and distant mountains. Bird watching, loch/sea fishing, walking, safe beaches, or just sit relaxing. For the fortunate, seals and otters can be seen in the adjacent bay. The two acre site's perimeter is fenced, making it safe for pets and children, always welcome. Helpful and friendly atmosphere. All accommodation fully equipped except linen. Tourist Board member. Open February to December. Weekly terms from £95 inclusive (caravan); £150 (house). SAE or phone for details.

CARAVAN SITES AND NIGHT HALTS

MUIR OF ORD. 🚐 💲 𝐀 **Mrs M.C. Stewart, Druimorrin Caravan and Camping Park, Urray, Muir of Ord IV6 7UL (099-73 252).** On A832 two miles west of Muir of Ord, this small quiet and pleasant touring site is owned and operated personally by the Stewart family, whose aim is to maintain the highest standards possible. Within easy touring reach of Loch Ness, Skye, Easter and Wester Ross. Excellent fishing, pony trekking, hill walking and bird watching, wild flowers and fossil grounds of an equal standard in the Black Isle. Modern four-berth caravans for hire fully equipped including bed linen, also laundry, shop, toilets, showers and dish washing facilities. Children and dogs under control are most welcome.

SHIELBRIDGE (Glen Shiel). 💲 𝐀 **Shiel Caravan Site, Shielbridge, by Kyle.** Touring site situated at the west end of the spectacular Glen Shiel, on the A87 Fort William to Kyle of Lochalsh road (access by shop at Shielbridge). This is an ideal centre from which to explore the beautiful West Coast, and is 15 miles from the Isle of Skye ferry at Kyle. There is space for 25 caravans and 50 tents; all usual facilities including showers with free hot water. Shop and snack bar adjacent, gas and petrol available. The site is Tourist Board registered, and open from Easter to October. Children and pets welcome. Rates from £2 per person per night. For further details, contact: **Dochfour Estate Office, Dochgarroch, Inverness IV3 6JP (0463 86 295).**

STIRLINGSHIRE

CARAVAN SITES AND NIGHT HALTS

STIRLING by. 🚐 💲 𝐀 **Auchenbowie Caravan Site, By Stirling FK7 8HE (0324 822141).** Peaceful central situation in rural surroundings, offering an ideal base for touring. Pitches for caravans, motor caravans and tents. Electric hook-ups available. Comfortable, well kept static caravans also available. Open April to October. Please write or telephone for further information.

WIGTOWNSHIRE

CARAVANS FOR HIRE

LUCE BAY. 🚐 💲 𝐀 **Cock Inn Caravan Park, Luce Bay.** √ √ √ √ Thistle Award. Get away from it all at a peaceful, select Caravan Park adjacent to a pleasant little beach and small Country Inn. Panoramic view across beautiful Luce Bay. Ideal location for sailing, bathing, sea-angling, beachcombing, etc. Golf, pony trekking and fishing are all available nearby. Park has modern toilet block, showers, shaver points and all facilities. FULLY SERVICED HOLIDAY CARAVANS FOR HIRE: TOURERS WELCOME — ELECTRIC HOOK-UPS AVAILABLE. Static caravans accommodate six persons. Shop on site; Bar Meals can be obtained at the Inn. There is also a BUNGALOW available all year round. Terms for static caravans range from £120 to £215 weekly; tourers from £6.00 to £8.50. Location: at Auchenmalg, A747 Glenluce/Port William Road, five miles from Glenluce. Please send SAE for brochure to: **Cock Inn Caravan Park, Auchenmalg, Newton Stewart, Wigtownshire DG8 0JH (0581 500227).**

PORT WILLIAM. 🔲 **Auchness Farm Caravan Park, Port William.** Mobile homes, on Auchness Caravan Park, just off B7021, consisting of three bedrooms, bathroom with flush toilet, washbasin and shower, full gas cooker, fire and water heater, electric lights, fridge and TV. Vans fully equipped including linen and cutlery. Gas and electricity provided. Some brand new homes available. Play area for small children and access to private swimming pool. Pony trekking nearby and bowls, tennis, fishing are available at Port William and Whithorn/Isle of Whithorn, also golf course at Monreith where there are safe sandy beaches. Historic dig at Whithorn. St. Ninian established the first church in this area. Terms from £100 per week. Please apply to: **Mrs E. Walker, Barwinnock Farm, Whauphill DG8 9PX (Port William [098-87] 291).**

HOLIDAY PARKS AND CENTRES

STRANRAER. ☼ **Drumlochart Caravan Park, Lochnaw, Near Stranraer DG9 0RN (0776 870232. Fax: 0766 870276).** RAC appointed. AA four Pennants. British Holiday Parks √ √ √ √ √. Off the beaten track in an outstandingly beautiful glen, amidst 22 acres of rhododendron and birch, yet only four miles from Stranraer, eight from Portpatrick. Luxury fully serviced "Thistle" award winning six-berth caravans and chalets for rental from £135 to £278 per week. Fully equipped including colour TV and microwave. Fly fishing on own 10-acre loch, regularly stocked with rainbow trout. Licensed lounge bar, heated swimming pool, children's play park, shop and launderette. Sea fishing, horse riding and first class golf courses very near. **Write or phone for colour brochure.** A718 from Stranraer, left on B7043 at Leswalt; 1½ miles. Park on right.

CARAVAN SITES AND NIGHT HALTS

NEWTON STEWART. 🅂 **Mr R. Wither, Creebridge Caravan Park, Newton Stewart DG8 6AJ (0671 2324).** A level four acre urban site offering 36 touring pitches and 50 statics. Security street lighting on site. Situated only a short walk from the amenities of the town centre, bowling green nearby. Quarter of a mile east of Newton Stewart off the A75. Open March to October. Fees on application.

NEWTON STEWART. 🚐 🅂 🅰 **Mrs B. McNeill, Creetown Caravan Park, Silver Street, Creetown, Newton Stewart DG8 7HU (067182 377).** √ √ √ √ Clean, modern, well-run, flat, grassy site with facilities for tourers and tents; also luxury caravan for hire. Amenities include excellent toilet block with showers, launderette; heated outdoor swimming/paddling pool; games room; children's play area. Within a short walk of village and its facilities. New and used caravans for sale. Pets welcome. Terms: £7 to £8 nightly for tourers, £100 to £150 per week for statics. Off season reductions available.

ORKNEY ISLES

CARAVANS FOR HIRE

WESTRAY. 🚐 **Mrs Seatter, Mount Pleasant, Westray KW17 2DH (08577 229).** Come and relax on this beautiful island. Lovely sandy beach only five minutes' walk from the caravans, ideal for children. Five minutes' walk to the shops. Visit Noltland Castle, built for Mary Queen of Scots, or watch the birds on the cliffs and seals on the water. Bicycles and cars for hire on the island and there is also an indoor swimming pool. Boat available for hire to the next island where there are archaeological sites of great interest. Three caravans for hire, all linen provided. From £60 per week. For more particulars please telephone.

CARAVAN SITES AND NIGHT HALTS

KIRKWALL. 🅂 🅰 **Pickaquoy Camping and Caravan Site, Kirkwall, Orkney.** √ √ √ √ Pickaquoy is situated on the outskirts of Kirkwall, a town with a population of 6500. The site is sheltered with extensive plantings and is on the edge of an open park with an adjacent children's play area and the sea close by. There are 30 pitches for campers and touring caravans. Electric hook-ups. The amenity block provides showers, laundry and washing-up facilities, along with irons, hairdryers and public telephone. Costs range from £2.10 for a small tent to £4.50 for caravans. Sorry, no dogs. Directions: turn right off A965 on entering Kirkwall from the west. For full details contact: **Department of Education and Recreation Services, Orkney Islands Council, Kirkwall, Orkney KW15 1NY (0856 873535, extension 2404).**

STROMNESS. 🅂 🅰 **Point of Ness Camping and Caravan Site, Stromness.** √ √ √ This site is on the outskirts of the small, attractive town of Stromness and is surrounded by sea on two sides. The site is grassy, with 30 pitches for campers and touring caravans. A new amenity block provides showers, laundry and washing-up facilities, iron and hairdryers. Electric hook-ups. There is a picturesque golf course close by. Costs range from £2.10 for a small tent to £4.50 for caravans. Sorry, no dogs. Directions: for walkers, follow Main Street south; vehicles, follow signposted route. For details contact: **Department of Education and Recreation Services, Orkney Islands Council, Kirkwall, Orkney KW15 1NY (0856 873535).**

🚐 Caravans for Hire (one or more caravans for hire on a site)

☼ Holiday Parks & Centres (usually larger sites hiring holiday homes/vans, with amenities)

🅂 Caravan Sites (for touring caravans, caravanettes, etc.)

🅰 Camping Sites (where campers are welcome)

WALES

CLWYD

CARAVANS FOR HIRE

ABERGELE. 📞 **Mr and Mrs T.P. Williams, Pen Isaf Caravan Park, Llangernyw, Abergele LL22 8RN (Llangernyw [074-576] 276).** This small caravan site is in beautiful unspoilt countryside, ideal for touring North Wales and situated 10 miles from the coast and 12 miles from Betws-y-Coed. The eight-berth caravans are fully equipped except for linen and towels and have shower, flush toilets, hot and cold water, Calor gas cooker, electric light and fridge. Fresh eggs and milk can be obtained from the farm on which this 20-caravan site is situated. Children especially will enjoy a holiday here, there being ample play space and facilities for fishing and pony riding. Pets are allowed but must be kept under control. Open from March to October. Terms on application. SAE please.

RUTHIN. 📞 **Mrs E. Jones, Tyddyn Isaf, Rhewl, Ruthin LL15 1UH (0824 703367).** One six-berth caravan situated in its own surroundings on an 80-acre working mixed farm. Three miles from market town of Ruthin, convenient for visiting Chester, coast or Snowdonia. It has one double and one twin bedroom, both with continental quilts; bathroom with flush toilet; kitchen/diner with three ring electric cooker, fridge, spin dryer; lounge with electric fire, colour TV and double sofa bed. Children Welcome. Sorry no pets. 50p electric meter. Available from Whitsun to October from £75 weekly.

DYFED

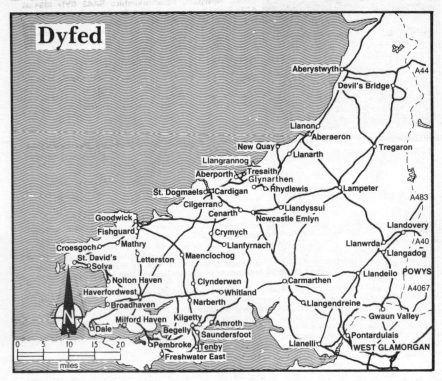

CARAVANS FOR HIRE

ABERYSTWYTH. 🚐 **Mrs Anne Bunton, Cwmergyr Farm, Ponterwyd, Aberystwyth SY23 3LB (097-085 301).** This luxury six-berth caravan is set in its own enclosure on a 250-acre sheep farm in the beautiful Cambrian Mountains, 16 miles east of Aberystwyth, off the A44. Accommodation consists of two bedrooms, bathroom with flush toilet, vanity unit and shower, kitchen with fridge and gas cooker, spacious lounge with colour TV and gas fire. Hot and cold water throughout. Spectacular views. Guests must bring own linen. Sorry, no pets. A car is essential, ample parking. Within a 15-mile radius there are sandy beaches, opportunities for fishing, golf, pony trekking; steam railway to visit, scenic drives and walks. This is an ideal base for exploring mid-Wales. On site, there is a stream and farm animals which the children will love. Open from 1st April to 31st October. Terms from £95 to £115 per week, inclusive of all gas and electricity.

ABERYSTWYTH AREA. 🚐 **Mrs A. Pugh, Talwrn Coch Farm, Llanrhystud SY23 5EL (Nebo [0974] 272214).** A six-berth caravan on a dairy/sheep farm, 12 miles from the university/holiday town of Aberystwyth and nine miles from the picturesque fishing resort of Aberaeron. The farm is in a quiet position near open moorland but is only three miles from Cardigan Bay and the safe bathing beach at Llanrhystud. Many more lovely beaches within an easy drive and pony trekking is available locally. The caravan is fully equipped, except for linen, and has a flush toilet and TV. Cot available on request. Fresh milk available. Children especially welcome. Well behaved pets welcome. Price from £50 per week. SAE for further details. FHG Diploma 1988.

FISHGUARD BAY.  **N. and L. Harries, Fishguard Bay Caravan and Camping Park, Dinas Cross, Newport, Pembrokeshire SA42 0YD (03486 415).** Enjoy a stay at our quiet, family-run Park situated on this beautiful stretch of Pembrokeshire National Park coastline. Ideal as a centre for walking and touring. The coast path leads off in both directions affording excellent walks along this stretch of 'Heritage' coast. Modern holiday caravans equipped to high standards are available, all carefully situated to enjoy the view. Touring caravans, motor caravans and tents are welcome. Some pitches have electrical hook-ups. Amenities include shop, launderette, small children's play area, games room and television room. There is access down to the shingle cove, picnic area and viewpoint.

HAVERFORDWEST.  **Scamford Caravan Park, Keeston, Haverfordwest, Pembrokeshire SA62 6HN (0437 710304).** √√√√√ **Dragon Award.** 25 Dragon Award luxury holiday caravans on peaceful park in attractive countryside, near Pembrokeshire Coastal Path and many lovely beaches. Every caravan has all mains services, fridge, gas fire, shower, colour TV. Also five touring pitches with electric hook-ups. Free hot showers. Excellent children's playground with swings, sandpit, climbing frame and trampoline. Dog welcome. Some caravans "dog-free" for the sake of children with allergies. Telephone. Launderette, with ironing facilities. Lots to do in the area — castles, farm parks, craft shops, boat trips, island bird sanctuaries, surfing, golf, riding, etc., or spend a day at Oakwood Leisure Park with its many attractions. Colour brochure from resident owners **Jean and Maurice Gould.**

LETTERSTON. **Sue Burnett, Swmbarch House, Letterston, Haverfordwest SA62 5UE (0348 840495).** Caravan for two adults plus two/four children situated in the heart of the beautiful West Wales countryside. 15 miles from the ancient cathedral city of St. Davids; eight miles from coast and central to the uncrowded, sandy beaches and the county's many other attractions. Come and explore Pembrokeshire at your leisure. The caravan shares a small paddock with ducks, rabbits and guinea pigs at our family home. Relaxed atmosphere, ideal for children. All services, but no TV! Shower, washing machine and tumble dryer available. No dogs please. From £80 per week. Write or phone for details.

PENDINE. **Mr H. Owen, The Grove Caravan Park, Pendine (09945 496).** Sited in a quiet woodland area. We are three-quarters of a mile from Pendine Beach and one mile from footpath to the beach at Morfa Bychan. Touring caravans and campers welcome. All modern conveniences on site including showers and toilets, and a launderette. Caravans for hire with all mains services. Open April to October.

SARNAU. **Mr and Mrs G. and E. Griffiths, Treddafydd, Sarnau, Llandyssul SA44 6PZ (Llangranog [0239] 654551).** Treddafydd Farm Caravan site is a small quiet site, situated just one mile from the sandy Penbryn Beach. Children are most welcome to see and enjoy life on this working dairy farm. All of the modern six-berth caravans for hire have hot and cold water, toilet and shower. A car is essential. The site is open from April to October with sites for tourers and campers also available. Tumble dryer, washing machine, spin dryer and ironing facilities. Prices from £80 to £220. SAE for free brochure.

SAUNDERSFOOT. **Bonvilles Court Caravan Site, Saundersfoot.** Occupying a pleasant site five minutes from the beach and harbour there are very comfortable six-berth caravans. An ideal place for children, a well-drained grassy site surrounded by shrubs and trees. A select position, sunny and quiet, with tarmac approach road. Vans are fully equipped except for sheets. They have Calor gas cookers, fridges, mains water, electric lighting and colour TV. Caravans with hot running water and shower or bath. On site there are showers and toilets conveniently placed. Pets welcome under control. Excellent choice of sandy beaches. Tenby and Amroth three miles, Wiseman's Bridge two; boating, sailing, amusements within easy reach. Excellent walks, bird sanctuaries, regular sailings from Tenby to Caldey Island. Terms and particulars from: **Mr D.R. Williams, Cloth Hall, Llanboidy, Whitland SA34 0EJ (0994 448 364).**

A GUIDE TO RECOGNISED CARAVAN HOLIDAY GRADING SYMBOLS

From *Approved* (√ or √ √) through *Good* and *Very Good* to *Excellent* (√ √ √ √ √), these are the symbols of the BRITISH HOLIDAY PARKS GRADING SCHEME. Operated throughout Britain by the British Holiday and Home Parks Association, the National Caravan Council and the English, Scottish and Wales Tourist Boards, the scheme covers the quality, standards and cleanliness of the park and its facilities.

In Wales, the DRAGON AWARD caravans are inspected annually to ensure that they meet exacting criteria of accommodation and amenity. A Dragon Award guarantees high levels of comfort and convenience.

HOLIDAY PARKS AND CENTRES

ABERYSTWYTH. 🚐 ☼ 💲 🅰 **Mr A.P. Ballard, Aberystwyth Holiday Village, Penparcau Road, Aberystwyth SY23 1BP (0970 624211).** A great place for a family holiday. Situated in six acres of land with panoramic views of Aberystwyth, Cardigan Bay and the Rheidol Valley. The site can accommodate tourers, tents and has static caravans. Facilities include club entertainment, heated pool, café/takeaway, amusements, play area, shop, laundry, etc. Nearby there is fishing, sailing, canoeing, horse riding, golf, swimming and much more. Open March to October. Big discounts for off-season bookings.

CARDIGAN. 🚐 ☼ 💲 🅰 **Mrs Y.M. Davies, Cenarth Falls Holiday Park, Cenarth, Newcastle Emlyn SA38 9JS (0239 710345).** √ √ √ √ √ Family

run park in beautiful country setting in the heart of the Teifi Valley with fishing available close by. Only a short drive to great beaches and coastal activities. All caravan accommodation to the very highest standards of cleanliness and comfort carrying "Dragon Award" status. WTB √ √ √ √ √ (Excellent) Graded Park. Facilities include outdoor heated swimming pool and sun patio, children's play area and indoor games room, mini market, character clubhouse featuring live entertainment on selected dates. Ideal for a relaxing, away from it all holiday but with plenty to see and do for the more energetic. Touring caravans are also welcome.

🚐 Caravans for Hire (one or more caravans for hire on a site)

☼ Holiday Parks & Centres (usually larger sites hiring holiday homes/vans, with amenities)

💲 Caravan Sites (for touring caravans, caravanettes, etc.)

🅰 Camping Sites (where campers are welcome)

HAVERFORDWEST. ☼ **Broad Haven Holiday Park, Haverfordwest SA62 3JD (0437 781277; Fax: 0437 781088).** ✓ ✓ ✓ ✓ Whatever your interest, Pembrokeshire has something to offer you and your family. On site you will find a playground, launderette and shop. Within easy walking distance the local villages offer a number of fine hostelries. The Dragon Award caravan holiday homes lack none of the comforts of home, with up to three bedrooms, kitchen, toilet and shower, electric lighting, piped gas, mains water and drainage. For our free colour brochure please telephone.

BROAD HAVEN HOLIDAY •PARK•

HAVERFORDWEST near (Little Haven). 🚐 ☼ 💲 **Hasguard Cross Caravan Park, Little Haven, Near Haverfordwest SA62 3SL (Broad Haven [0437] 781443).** ✓ ✓ ✓ ✓ AA three Pennants. Open all year. Set in three and a quarter acres of level grassland tastefully screened by trees and shrubs with views overlooking Milford Haven and St. Bride's Bay. The park caters for static and touring caravans. All the usual facilities are available including licensed club with extensive bar snack menu. The park is situated on the Dale Peninsula in the centre of the Pembrokeshire Coast National Park, surrounded by rocky bays and sandy beaches. Every holiday attraction is available nearby. Terms from £85 weekly. From Haverfordwest take B4327 for seven miles. Write or phone for brochure.

TENBY near. 🚐 Luxury six-berth caravan, three miles from picturesque Tenby. Lydstep offers a quiet and restful holiday amid lovely surroundings whilst providing for all the family's needs. Entertainment is available on site, also swimming pool, play areas etc. Breathtaking views of the bay and Caldey Island. For details contact **Mrs E. Neville, 283 Iffley Road, Oxford, Oxfordshire OX4 4AQ (0865 727669).**

CARAVAN SITES AND NIGHT HALTS

AMROTH. 🚐 💲 🏕 **Mr A.A. Lewis, Little Kings Park, Amroth SA67 8PG (Llanteg [083-483] 330).** Small family site overlooking sea and beautiful views. Twenty three-bedroomed 35ft caravans for hire. Thirty-five touring caravans all with electric hook-up and camping for 50. Level site and enclosed heated swimming pool, patio bar, games and pool rooms, launderette, children's play area. New modern shower/toilet block with washing-up room. Ideal centre for exploring Pembrokeshire — castles, beautiful beaches. Tenby and Saundersfoot nearby. Take A477 from St. Clears at left signpost to Amroth/Ludchurch (approximately 8 miles); continue along this road at signpost Ludchurch/Narbeth turn right. Site quarter mile on left. Colour brochure available on request.

HAVERFORDWEST. 💲 🏕 **Mrs F.M. Rowe, Rhyndaston, Hayscastle, Haverfordwest SA62 5PT (0438 840272).** This is a small, secluded site in very attractive surroundings, a quiet valley with a trout stream. This is the ideal situation for the true country lover. Touring vans/campers are welcome; terms from £3.00 to £5.25. Hot water/showers on site. Car essential to get the most from your holiday. Children welcome, pets accepted. Take A487 from Haverfordwest, turn right at Rock Motel; signposted from turning.

NORTH PEMBROKESHIRE. 🚐 **Mrs T. Jones, Penbanc, Tegryn, Llanfyrnach, Pembrokeshire SA35 0BP (023-977 279/666).** Working family farm with sheep, cows, calves, ponies, free-range hens, ducks, geese and, sometimes, pigs. We offer an eight-berth caravan in its own paddock near the farmyard, with lovely views. Facilities include shower, flush toilet, fridge, Calor gas cooker, heater, colour TV and picnic table. Centrally based for walking, touring, trekking and birdwatching. Coast 20 minutes by car (essential) with sandy beaches, rocky coves, Coastal Path and islands to visit. Lots of fishing — sea, reservoir, river and farm pool. Plenty to do: castles, museums, crafts centres, nature reserves, theme park, zoo, leisure centre, swimming pools, steam trains — a wide variety of activities. Caravan available May to September. We can also offer a self-contained half of farmhouse, sleeps six plus cot. Details on request.

TENBY. 🚐 💲 🏕 **Miss Aileen Sole, Hazelbrook Caravan Park, Sageston, Tenby SA70 8SY (Carew [0646] 651351).** Four, six and eight-berth caravans for hire. A quiet country park five miles from Tenby with easy access for touring the beautiful Pembrokeshire coast and countryside. One mile from Carew Castle and river, and a restored watermill. A family run park with a friendly atmosphere. Games room, off-licence, launderette, electric hook-ups and with free showers available. Pets welcome. Touring pitches available. Tourist Board registered. Hire vans from £20 per night.

SOUTH GLAMORGAN

HOLIDAY PARKS AND CENTRES

RHOOSE. 🚐 ☼ 💲 **Fontgary Holiday Leisure Park, Rhoose CF6 9ZT (Tel: 0446 710386; Fax: 0446 710613).** Fontgary Holiday Park is situated beside the Bristol Channel in the rural Vale of Glamorgan. High quality facilities include superb 25 metre indoor heated pool with funpool, poolside snackbar, cabaret lounge bars, shop, hairdresser, children's fun centre, games room and unique octagonal restaurant. Our superbly equipped health club is available for temporary membership. This beautifully kept park is ideal for visiting the numerous attractions in the area. Luxury Dragon Award Caravan Holiday Homes with colour TVs are available with a choice of either two or three bedrooms. Touring Caravans welcome — sorry, no tents. Send or telephone for your free colour brochure.

CARAVAN SITES AND NIGHT HALTS

COWBRIDGE. 💲 **Llandow Touring Caravan Park, Llandow, Cowbridge CF7 7PB (0446 794527).** √ √ √ A warm friendly welcome awaits you when you visit Llandow Touring Caravan Park, set in the Vale of Glamorgan, halfway between the market town of Cowbridge and the historic town of Llantwit Major, three miles from the beautiful Heritage Coast and within easy reach of Cardiff. Our modern spotless amenities include FREE hot showers, hot water, clothes and dish washing facilities and children's play area. The level, free-draining park has electric hook-ups, shop, gas and laundry. Pets welcome if kept on lead. Separate rally field and storage available. AA three Pennants; RAC Appointed; BH&HPA members. Terms on request.

GWENT

CARAVAN SITES AND NIGHT HALTS

MONMOUTH. 🚐 💲 Å **Mr S.A. Holmes, Bridge Caravan Park and Camping Site, Dingestow, Monmouth NP5 4DY (060083 241).** √ √ √ √ √ In the heart of the Vale of Usk and Wye Valley, set in the small village of Dingestow four miles from Monmouth and three miles from Raglan. Visitors can choose to spend time simply relaxing in the quiet surroundings or take advantage of the multitude of activities in the area — fishing, golf, walking, pony trekking, leisure centres, etc. Excellent site facilities. Dogs allowed if kept on leads. Terms from £5 per night per touring caravan; £100 per week per hired static caravan. Open from Easter to end October. Brochure available. AA three Pennants.

GWYNEDD

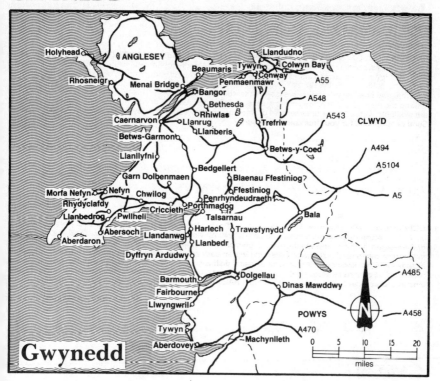

Gwynedd

CARAVANS FOR HIRE

ANGLESEY. 🚐 💲 ⛺ **Mr B.W. Jones, Nant Newydd Caravan Park, Brynteg, Near Benllech Bay, Anglesey LL78 7JH (0248 852842 or 852266).**

√ √ √ √ √ Caravans for hire on small select countryside site, two and a half miles from Benllech Bay. All facilities; showers, toilets, washers, dryers, irons, hairdryers, and hot water 24 hours a day. Outdoor heated swimming pool, games room, Satellite TV and large play area plus small play area for under 5's. Licensed shop, telephone, first aid room. Tents and tourers especially welcome. Pitches with hard standings, mains water, electricity. Pony trekking, golf, fishing, water ski-ing, climbing, etc all within three miles. 5 Pennants Dragon Award. Runner-up to best park in Wales for two years running. AA, RAC Approved; NCC Member; BH&HPA Member. Terms and brochure on request.

BALA. 🚐 **Mrs S.E. Edwards, Bryn Melyn Farm, Rhyduchaf, Bala LL23 7PG (Bala [0678] 520376).** One six-berth caravan is available on Bryn Melyn, a 56 acre mixed farm in the village of Rhyduchaf, two miles from Bala, situated in the beautiful Bala countryside. The caravan has a bathroom, inside flush toilet, hot and cold water, electric light, gas cooker, gas heater, fridge, colour TV. Fully equipped with blankets etc. Children are welcome. Sorry no pets allowed. Open from April to September. Seaside 25 miles away. Weekly rates from £75 (reduced for Senior Citizens May, June and September). Electricity on slot meter (10p). SAE, please, for further details.

BENLLECH. 🚐 💲 ⛺ **Golden Sunset Holidays, Benllech Bay, Anglesey LL74 8SW (0248 852345).** Beautiful caravan and camping park overlooking the sea with miles of glorious sands and safe bathing. Modern caravans for hire each having flush toilet and shower. Farmhouse and bungalow to rent. Touring caravans welcome. Organised camps for schools, Scouts, Guides, etc., are catered for, having their own separate well sheltered fields with mains water and full facilities. Special quotations on request. The village of Benllech has a good range of shops, a post office and launderette. Dogs on lead only. Donkey rides for children. Pony rides for adults and children. Open April to end of September. Send for free brochure.

CRICCIETH. 🚐 🅢 **Mrs L. Hughes Jones, Tyddyn Heilyn Farm, Chwilog LL53 6SW (0766 810441).** √ √ √ √

On a small farm site, in beautiful tranquil countryside, a luxurious and spacious caravan with a shower room, well equipped kitchen, comfortable lounge/diner with colour TV. It can sleep up to 6 persons — duvets supplied. There is a small separate Caravan Park for tourers, motor caravans, and tents. It has flush toilets, hot/cold showers, electric hook-ups etc. The setting is level, sheltered and looking onto open country facing the Cambrian Coast, with beautiful Lon Goed Walks passing through our farmland which enjoys clean unpolluted sea and mountain air. It is ideal for sea sports, birdwatching as there are such a vast number of birds homed in the flowered hedgerows, quite near to two good fishing rivers, riding, golf, shooting, and climbing as we are on the edge of the Snowdonia National Park. A new leisure centre with the new Olympic yachting harbour is five minutes away. Also let for furnished holidays are a charming farm cottage, also a NORWEGIAN HOME able to sleep up to six persons and having 4 gradings. Please write or phone for more details and the moderate terms.

DOLGELLAU. 🚐 **E. Wynne-Williams, Coed Croes, Dolgellau LL40 1TD (0341 422658).** Modern and comfortable caravan, six/eight berth, situated on the foothills of Cader Idris Mountain, 40 yards from farmhouse. Hot and cold shower and basin, toilet; two separate bedrooms; bedding provided but bring own linen. Gas or electric heating, gas cooking, electric fridge and lighting (no meters), TV. Dolgellau town two miles, beach seven miles. All recreational activities and restaurants, etc within easy reach. Sorry, no pets. Very reasonable terms.

LLANBEDROG. 🚐 🅢 🏕 **Mrs L.O. Williams, Bodwrog Farm, Llanbedrog, Pwllheli LL53 7RE (Llanbedrog [0758] 740341).** One well-equipped Pemberton Cresta Villa 32 foot, six-berth, luxury caravan to let, Easter to end of October. The only static on mixed farm with stupendous coastal and mountain views. Sandy beach one-and-a-half miles. Clean and well-aired, the caravan is fully equipped with shower, washbasin, flush toilet, fridge, colour TV. Plenty of clean bedding; cot available (free occasional babysitting). Terms from £80 to £100 per week, according to season, INCLUDE electricity, gas and pillowcases. Sheets can be hired but are free for FORTNIGHT lets. One house-trained pet allowed. Free rough shooting on request for static caravan guests. "Special Breaks" available in April, early May and October. Also campsite with shower and toilet facilities, mains water and superb sea views; no overcrowding. Pub three quarters of a mile. Family tents £2.50 per night; caravanette £2.50; tourer caravan £2.50–£3 per night.

MOELFRE. 🚐 **Mrs G. Williams, Tyddyn Gwynt, Moelfre, Anglesey, Gwynedd LL72 8NN (Moelfre [024-888] 296).**

One six-berth caravan, situated in its own garden on a farm overlooking the sandy Lligwy beach, which is only about five minutes' walk from the farm. The caravan has two end bedrooms, one double room and one bunk room. It has hot and cold water, flush toilet, shower, TV, fridge, electric lighting, gas cooking and heating. Fully equipped except linen. Children are welcome and pets allowed if kept under control. Shop/bakery, post office, craft shops and pub in nearby Moelfre village. Full details on request.

PORTHMADOG. 🚐 **Mrs E.A.J. Williams, Tyddyn Deucwm Isaf, Penmorfa, Porthmadog LL49 9SD (Porthmadog [0766] 513683). Working farm.** Luxurious six-berth leisure home, between Criccieth and Porthmadog in Snowdonia National Park. Magnificent views of Cardigan Bay. Only one on quiet working farm. Elevated sunny position, about ten minutes from beach and near Snowdonia Mountains. Only five minutes from shop, pub, hotel and "take-away". Seven minutes from world famous Ffestiniog Narrow Gauge Railway, near riding and fishing. Walks nearby and also on the farm. Three separate bedrooms, electricity and gas, fridge, hot and cold water, shower and toilet, colour TV. Pets by arrangement. Meet Welsh Tourist Board standard. SAE or telephone, please state number in party.

GWYNEDD – OUTSTANDING NATURAL BEAUTY!
With Snowdonia National Park and the Lleyn Peninsula, Gwynedd well deserves its designation as an 'Area of Outstanding Natural Beauty'. The tourist is spoiled for choice in this county but should endeavour to visit the hill-fort at Tre'r Ceiri, the Llugwy Valley, Cwm Pennant, Dinas Dinlle hill-fort, the gold mine at Clogau and the railways and quarries at Blaenau Ffestiniog.

PWLLHELI. Mrs G.M. Pollard, Cefn Côch, Efailnewydd, Near Pwllheli LL53 5TP (0758 612270).

Forty-foot six-berth caravan pleasantly and privately situated in grounds of smallholding with panoramic views over open countryside. Central for Abersoch, Pwllheli, Nefyn, Lleyn Peninsula and Snowdonia. Three golf courses and sports centre close by. Accommodation comprises lounge with colour TV, convertible double bed settee, electric fire, french windows; kitchen/diner with cooker, fridge and sink; full bathroom (with bath); one double, one twin bedrooms. Garden furniture and barbecue. Visitors welcome to help in stable yard.

PWLLHELI. Mrs Catherine Jones, St. Tudwal's View, Pentreuchaf, Pwllheli LL53 8DZ (0758 750327). One six-berth static caravan situated on six acre farm on Llyn Peninsula. Panoramic views of mountains and Cardigan Bay, and only four miles from the beach. The caravan sleeps six in an end bedroom with double bed, second bedroom with two bunks, and a third room with double bed which converts to two singles. Own inside shower room, washbasin with hot and cold water, flush toilet. Fully equipped except for linen; electric light, cooker, kettle, fridge and fire; television; electricity on 50p meter. Cot available. Pets welcome. Plenty of parking space. Cleanliness and comfort guaranteed. SAE for terms and details.

HOLIDAY PARKS AND CENTRES

ANGLESEY. Mr and Mrs J.E. and E.W. Hunt, Tyddyn Isaf Caravan Park, Lligwy Bay, Dulas, Anglesey LL70 9PQ (0248 410203).

√ √ √ √ √ These first class luxury caravans have been awarded the Dragon Award by the Wales Tourist Board and the AA 4 Pennants for their site facilities. The eight-berth caravans have two and three bedrooms, cooker, fire, showers, flush toilets, hot and cold water, fridge and colour TV. The site facilities include sanitation, water, electricity, gas, site shop, swings, licensed club, take-away food and laundry facilities. The safe, sandy beach can be reached directly from the site (150 yards) and there are swimming baths aplenty on Anglesey. Golf, tennis, fishing, riding and bathing all within easy reach. Half an hour's drive to Snowdonia National Park. Open from 1st March to 31st October. Children welcome. Pets by arrangement. Terms from £100 weekly for holiday homes. Tourers from £8. Six acres for campers from £6 per tent.

See also Colour Display Advertisement **CAERNARFON.** Beach Holiday, West Point, The Beach, Pontllyfni, Caernarfon LL54 5ET (0286 660400). √ √ √ √ √ Our world by the sea offers you a choice of executive beach bungalow, villa chalet or luxury caravan, all situated in attractive surroundings. All are equipped to the highest standards. WTB Dragon Award. For further details and brochure telephone.

CARAVAN SITES AND NIGHT HALTS

ANGLESEY. 🅢 Å **Point Lynas Caravan Park, Llaneilian, Amlwch, Anglesey LL67 9LT (040 831130/0248 852423).** Quiet sea edge park at north-east corner of Anglesey, overlooking Point Lynas. Two well-kept level enclosures for tents, tourers, or motor caravans, one with sea views, the other more sheltered. Each enclosure accommodates eight or nine units and is close to our modern purpose-built amenity block. Ladies' and gents', utility room with showers, laundry, and utensil washing facilities. Waste water disposal point. Electric hook-ups available. Porth Eilian Cove 200 metres, safe for swimming, fishing; small slipway for launching boats. Shop in Amlwch one and a half mile away.

POINT LYNAS CARAVAN PARK

BALA. 🏠 Å **Mrs O. Davies, Rhydydefaid Farm, Frongoch, Bala LL23 7NT (0678 520 456** Situated in grounds of a beef rearing farm, in its own private orchard with stream. Six-berth caravan, only three mile from Bala, near A4212 road. The accommodation consists one double bedroom, one room with bunk beds, and the seats form extra beds. Kitchen with fridge, gas cooke lounge/diner with gas heating. Shower etc. No linen or vided. Gas and electricity included in rent. A pet is allowe Placed centrally it can be used as a base to explore Snow donia and mid-Wales. The National White Water Centre one mile away, and camping with toilet/shower is availab on our farm.

CAERNARFON. 🛒 𝐀 **Ty'n yr Onnen Mountain Farm Park, Ty'n yr Onnen, Waunfawr, Caernarfon LL55 4AX (0286 650281).** √ √ √ √ AA Two Pennants. A 200-acre working farm at the foot of Moel Eilio in the Sowdonia Range. The perfect area for walks/tours in this most unspoilt and scenic part of Wales. The camping site is secluded and peaceful, with play/rest facilities and also opportunity for barbecues. You will enjoy the tranquillity of the valleys. We provide all modern facilities including electric hook-ups, rest room, laundry and wash-up room, as well as a shop, colour TV, pool tables, video machines, children's play park and small animals. The site is personally supervised and the owners take great pride in the cleanliness of the toilets and showers. Pets welcome. Prices from £5.00 per night for tent plus two people. Send SAE for our brochure.

CAERNARVON. 🚐 🛒 𝐀 **Mr and Mrs T.D. Onions, White Tower Caravan Park, Llandwrog, Caernarvon, Gwynedd LL54 5UH (0286 830649).** √ √ √ √ **National Grading.** AA 3 Pennants. Quiet family site giving splendid views of Snowdonia, yet only three miles from Caernarvon and two-and-a-half miles from the beach at Dinas Dinlle. Tourers and tents welcome, level touring field with 32 E/H and FREE hot showers. Heated swimming pool, Play area, Family bar, Shop, Launderette, and TV/Games room. All personally supervised by ourselves. Horseriding, golf, and all watersports (tuition available). Boat launching facilities and sea fishing all nearby. Our static park has modern caravans for sale and hire. *Directions:* south on the A487 from Caernarvon, after passing Leo's supermarket take the second turning right, signposted SARON 2 miles. Follow lane for 3 miles, site on right-hand side.

WHITE TOWER
CARAVAN
PARK
Nr. Caernarfon

CRICCIETH. 🛒 𝐀 **Mrs S.J. Jones, Maes Meillion, Llwyn Mafon Isaf, Criccieth LL52 0RE (Garn Dolbenmaen [076-675] 205).** Llwyn Mafon is a quiet select caravan site overlooking Cardigan Bay — panoramic view. Snowdon Mountain Range at rear. On main Porthmadog-Caernarfon road, the A487. Porthmadog and Criccieth three-and-a-half miles. Highly recommended. Limited to 20 caravans. Mains water, toilets, shower, mains electricity and shaving point. Limited number of hook-up electric connections. The sea is three-and-a-half miles. Children welcome and pets are allowed (under control). Advance booking advisable Easter to October. Rates for touring caravans from £5.50 per night; also weekly terms £35 plus £1 electricity per day. Please send SAE for brochure.

CRICCIETH. 🛒 𝐀 **Cae Canol Caravan and Camping Park, Cae Canol Farm, Criccieth LL52 0NB [0766 522351).** Situated on B4411, approximately one and a half miles north of Criccieth in an ideal position for exploring the area. This family site is flat, sheltered and easily accessible, with new, modern facilities including hot/cold water, ladies' and gents' showers. Electric hook-up points to all units; Calor gas cylinders exchanged. Pony rides, golf, etc within easy reach. Free fishing available (subject to WRA licence). Open April to October. Terms: Caravan £4 to £6.50; awnings FREE; Tent £3.50 to £5.00. Electric hook-up £1.50. AA two star; Local Authority licensed.

DOLGELLAU. 🛒 𝐀 **Mrs S.J. Lane, Llwyn-Yr-Helm Farm, Brithdir, Dolgellau LL40 2SR (Rhydymain [0341-41] 254).** Situated on a minor road half-a-mile off B4416, this is a quiet, small working farm site, four miles from Dolgellau in beautiful countryside, ideal for walking. Many places of interest in area including slate mines, narrow gauge railways, lakes and mountains and nine miles from sandy beaches. Toilet block and showers with free hot water; shaving points and plug. Small shop. Caravans, Dormobiles and tents, and electric hook-ups. Pets welcome. Open Easter to November. WTB verified.

FREE and REDUCED RATE Holiday Visits!
Don't miss our Reader's Offer Vouchers
on pages 13 to 31.

CAMPING SITES

CAERNARVON. 🔊 Å **Mrs Brenda E. Hummel, Riverside Camping, Caer Glyddyn, Pontrug, Caernarvon LL55 2BB (0286 678781; Fax: 0286 672524).** Sheltered four-and-a-half acre field, bordered by a lovely salmon river, provides an informal and peaceful site, situated two miles from Caernarvon on the right hand side of the A4086 (Caernarvon to Llanberis road), five miles from Llanberis in the heart of Snowdonia — ideal walking country. Railway Station at Bangor (10 miles), regular bus service from Caernarvon to Bangor and Llanberis. The river is a great attraction for boating, swimming and salmon fishing (permit only) in season. Near sea and mountains. The site has electric hook-ups, toilet and washing facilities, and is suitable for wheelchair access. Small playground. Milk delivered daily. General shop, launderette one mile away. Children welcome and well-controlled dogs permitted (must be kept on lead at all times). Touring caravans £6; small tent £2; large £5. Open Easter to October. Many castles, miniature railways, craft centres and gardens to visit in the area, also great range of outdoor activities including fishing, swimming, walking, climbing, riding and golf. AA one Pennant.

MACHYNLLETH near. 📺 🔊 Å **M. and I. Pugh, 'Ty'n-y-Pwll' Caravan and Camping Site, Dinas Mawddwy, Near Machynlleth, Powys SY20 9AF (0650 531326).** Two six-berth CARAVANS FOR HIRE and CAMPING facilities on level ground in a site on a lovely part of the Dovey Valley in the Snowdonia National Park. The Caravans have all amenities; toilet, TV, fridge, one with shaver. For campers, there are showers and flush toilets on site. Children and pets welcome. 'Yy'n-y-Pwll' is centrally situated for touring North and Mid-Wales and the coasts; Bala, Barmouth, Aberdovey, Fairbourne and Aberystwyth are all within easy reach. Lovely walks on the farm, and fishing for trout and salmon on the River Dovey. Climbers will find that they are well placed for Aran, Cader Idris and Snowdon mountains. SAE please for our very reasonable terms.

TAL-Y-LLYN, Tywyn. 🔊 Å **Dôl-Einion, Tal-y-Llyn, Tywyn LL36 9AJ (0654 761312).** Dôl-Einion is perhaps the prettiest camp site in the Snowdonia National Park. It is a flat three-acre meadow bordered by colourful rhododendrons in season and there is an attractive trout stream. The site nestles at the foot of mighty Cader Idris, at the start of the main path to the summit. Easy access on B4405 for caravans, camping vans. Good centre for walking or touring. Toilets and showers. Managed by resident owner. Terms on application.

POWYS

CARAVANS FOR HIRE

BRECON. 📺 🔊 Å **R. P.B. and W.P. Davies, Lakeside Caravan & Camping Site, Llangorse,**

Brecon LD3 7TR (Llangorse [087-484] 226). Lakeside Caravan & Camping Park, set next to Llangorse Lake in the heart of the fabulous Brecon Beacons National Park, is an ideal centre for touring in Wales or staying put and enjoying the many activities we have available. Fishing, hill walking, water ski-ing, pony trekking, sailing, canoeing and windsurfing. Slipway and jetty facilities. Heated pool. Launderette. Licensed Club. Restaurant and shop. Luxury caravans for hire from £125 per week — hot showers, flush toilets, TV, etc. All the facilities you would expect at our modern site in a rural setting. For brochure, SAE, please, **Ray and Wendy Davies**.

BUILTH WELLS. 📺 **Mrs P.A. Evans, Llwyn Farm, Aberedw, Builth Wells LD2 3YD (0982 570328).** Single six-berth mobile home for letting all year round. Situated in the beautiful Edw Valley which runs into upper reaches of the Wye with own panoramic views. On working mixed farm; fishing, ponies, wonderful walks. It has gas cooker and fire, electricity, fridge and TV; flush toilet (extra flush toilet, washbasin and shower nearby). Approached from Llandrindod Wells, Builth Wells or Hay-on-Wye, all nine miles away. Children and pets welcome. Very reasonable terms. For friendly, personal service please phone or write.

NEWTOWN. 📺 ☼ 🔊 **Gwernydd Caravan Park, New Mills, Newtown SY16 3NW (068 650236).** √ √ √ Quiet, secluded family-run retreat park standing on high ground, but in a sheltered position. Mostly south-facing views over beautiful countryside. A place to unwind from everyday pressures. Its location (A483 from Welshpool then right onto B4390) makes an ideal base from which to explore mountains, lakes and many beauty spots in this part of Wales. One hour's drive from the lovely beaches of the Cambrian coast. Close to Powys Castle, Llanfair Narrow Gauge Railway, situated between the market towns of Welshpool and Newtown. Pony trekking, fishing and golf close by. Licensed club; shop; laundry, showers, pay phone on site. Open March to November. Caravans for sale and hire.

HOLIDAY PARKS AND CENTRES

BUILTH WELLS. 🚐 ☼ 🍴 Å **Llewellyn Leisure Park, Cilmery, Builth Wells LD2 3NU (0831**

101052 or 0982 552838). √ √ √ RAC Appointed, AA, Caravan Club, Caravan & Camping Club Listings. Ideally situated for touring or peaceful relaxation in "secret" heart of Wales. Severn Bridge, Cardiff, Worcester and West/South Coast beaches all within one and a half hours' drive. Panoramic views towards Brecon Beacons from two-bedroomed modern luxury accommodation, including colour TV, from £117 to £279 weekly; sleeps 6 persons. Executive 31' × 12', including video, microwave, stereo, duvets from £178 to £348 weekly. Short Breaks available all season. Touring and camping from £6 to £9 per night; 240V electricity, water and drainage, hook-ups, hard standings. Adjacent Inn/Restaurant. Nearby facilities for fishing, golf, riding, bowls, tennis, swimming; theatre, sports centre, Wales Showground. Bed and Breakfast also offered at £16 per person per night. Conference facility for 30 persons. Under one hour to Brecon Beacons, Hay-on-Wye, Hereford and Elan Reservoirs. Convenient for Railway Station (200 yards) and bus services.

CARAVAN SITES AND NIGHT HALTS

BRECON. 🍴 Å **Mr and Mrs C.R. Jones, Brynich Caravan Park, Brecon LD3 7SH (0874 623325).** √ √ √ √ Brynich Caravan Park is a family run park at the foothills of the Brecon Beacons. Superbly situated one mile east of Brecon on the A470, near the junction with the A40. The site offers level pitches and a very clean modern toilet and amenity block with hot showers (all hot water free) including two disabled shower rooms, shaving and hair-drying points. Also electric hook-up points. There is a laundry room, public telephone, children's play area, baby changing room. Pets are welcome on a lead at all times and an exercise field is provided. The camp site shop stocks milk and gas and most requirements. An ideal base for the many walks nearby or to tour Mid and South Wales. AA Three Pennant site, RAC Appointed. Wales Tourist Board registered.

LLANGORSE. 🚐 🍴 **Llynfi Holiday Park, Llangorse.** √ √ √ Llynfi Holiday Park is a flat, well-sheltered grassland park at Llangorse Lake in the Brecon Beacons National Park. The facilities are first class and there is an excellent heated outdoor pool available to residents. Llynfi has its own boating slipway on to Llangorse Lake, where windsurfing, sailing, fishing and water ski-ing are permitted. Being situated in the middle of the Beacons and the Black Mountains Llynfi is in a very picturesque area of Britain and is a perfect base for touring South Wales and mid-Wales. The caravans for hire are all 30 feet in length and each has two bedrooms. Terms from £120 weekly. We can be reached from the A40 on to the B4560. SAE for details to: Llynfi Holiday Park, Llangorse Lake, Brecon, Powys LD3 7TR (087484 283).

NEWTOWN. 🍴 Å **Tynycwm Camping and Caravan Site, Aberhafesp, Newtown SY16 3JF (0686 88651).** A farm site on a level field with beautiful views. We enjoy showing visitors round the farm, which is ideal for children; families are particularly welcome. Pets are allowed but must be kept on a lead. Hot water and shower facilities are provided. Prices are from £5.00 per unit per night. We also have sites to let for holiday caravans. Nearest village three miles; pony trekking nearby. Find us seven miles NW of Newtown via A489 to Caersws, then B4569 North, signposted Aberhafesp. Cross the B4568 (ignoring the sign for Aberhafesp) and continue to the next crossroads. Turn left signposted Bwlch y Garreg. Farm and site one mile on the right. Grid Ref. 036 961.

IRELAND

ANTRIM

CARAVAN SITES AND NIGHT HALTS

ANTRIM. 💲 Å **Sixmilewater Caravan Park.** The Caravan Park is pleasantly landscaped and situate amongst mature trees close to the Lough Shore. There are scenic delights for holidaymakers of all kinds; i fact, anyone with time to spare and who appreciates natural beauty and tranquillity should not pass us b Facilities include modern toilet block, shower block, a fully equipped laundry and constant hot water. The sit accommodates touring caravans, motor vans and tents. Electric hook-up is available for half the berths o site. Why not send for our information brochure and enquire about prices for 1994? We will be delighted help you. **Antrim Borough Council, Leisure and Tourism Dept, The Steeple, Antrim BT41 1BJ.**

CORK

HOLIDAY PARKS AND CENTRES

CROOKHAVEN. 🚐 ☼ 💲 Å **Barleycove Caravan Park, Crookhaven, Co. Cork (010 353 2 35302 from outside Ireland, 028 35302 from Ireland**

Barleycove offers a choice of attractive mobile homes, area for tents and touring caravans. The Park has amenities whi include ultra-modern toilets and showers, mini-market, tak away, barbecue area, babysitting service. For the more activ holidaymakers there is tennis, pitch and putt, bicycles f hire, a games room and play areas for the children. Go fishing, water sports and lots of entertainment availab locally. Telephone for brochure.

🚐 Caravans for Hire (one or more caravans for hire on a site)

☼ Holiday Parks & Centres (usually larger sites hiring holiday homes/vans, with amenities)

💲 Caravan Sites (for touring caravans, caravanettes, etc.)

Å Camping Sites (where campers are welcome)

KERRY

HOLIDAY PARKS AND CENTRES

KILLORGLIN. ☼ ☼ **Liam and Linda West, West's Holiday Park, Killarney Road, Killorglin, Co. Kerry (066 61240; from Britain — 010 353 66 61240; Fax: 066 61833).** Scenic park which caters for everyone, with all facilities. Modern mobile homes for hire, Caravans, Dormobiles and Tents welcome. Just one mile from Killorglin on Ring of Kerry, on banks of River Laune renowned for trout and salmon fishing. Area is convenient for sandy beaches, all water sports and pastimes, squash, cycle hire, mountaineering, golf etc. Scenic drives all around, good choice of shops, restaurants, pubs. Central for touring Kerry. On site facilities include tennis court, children's swimming pool, play area, CTV lounge, sports opportunities, babysitting, shop, payphone, all usual facilities: showers, laundry room, etc. MCCI 5 star; Tourist Board 3 star. Prices from £89 to £279 for static caravan rental. Touring/camping rates on application. Send for our brochure.

CARAVAN SITES AND NIGHT HALTS

LAURAGH. 🏴 ⚑ **Creveen Lodge Caravan and Camping Park, Healy Pass Road, Lauragh (010 353 64 83131; from Ireland — 064 83131).** Our family-run small park, set in the heart of the beautiful scenery of south Kerry, with high standards of personal supervision, is fully serviced with excellent amenities. It is relaxing and well sheltered with easy access, walking or cycling, to forests, Caha Range of mountains, rivers, lakes and the famed Derreen Gardens. We are just one mile from the old Sibin Pub. Other activities nearby include river and sea angling, boating trips in Kenmare Bay. Open from Easter to 15th October. Charges all year £5.50 per unit nightly, 50p per person. Hikers and cyclists £2.50 per person. Electricity £1 per night. Weekly per unit £30.

FOR THE MUTUAL GUIDANCE
OF GUEST AND HOST

Every year literally thousands of holidays, short-breaks and overnight stops are arranged through our guides, the vast majority without any problems at all. In a handful of cases, however, difficulties do arise about bookings, which often could have been prevented from the outset.

It is important to remember that when accommodation has been booked, both parties — guests and hosts — have entered into a form of contract. We hope that the following points will provide helpful guidance.

GUESTS: When enquiring about accommodation, be as precise as possible. Give exact dates, numbers in your party and the ages of any children. State the number and type of rooms wanted and also what catering you require — bed and breakfast, full board, etc. Make sure that the position about evening meals is clear — and about pets, reductions for children or any other special points.

Read our reviews carefully to ensure that the proprietors you are going to contact can supply what you want. Ask for a letter confirming all arrangements, if possible.

If you have to cancel, do so as soon as possible. Proprietors do have the right to retain deposits and under certain circumstances to charge for cancelled holidays if adequate notice is not given and they cannot re-let the accommodation.

HOSTS: Give details about your facilities and about any special conditions. Explain your deposit system clearly and arrangements for cancellations, charges, etc, and whether or not your terms include VAT.

If for any reason you are unable to fulfil an agreed booking without adequate notice, you may be under an obligation to arrange alternative suitable accommodation or to make some form of compensation.

While every effort is made to ensure accuracy, we regret that FHG Publications cannot accept responsibility for errors, omissions or misrepresentation in our entries or any consequences thereof. Prices in particular should be checked because we go to press early. We will follow up complaints but cannot act as arbiters or agents for either party.

WEXFORD

CARAVAN SITES AND NIGHT HALTS

KILMUCKRIDGE. 💲 🅰 **Morriscastle Strand Caravan and Camping Park, Kilmuckridge (053**

30212, off season 01 535355; Fax: 01 545916). This site has been operated by the same family for 25 years, but has been regularly refurbished and now caters for up to 100 touring vans, with pitches spread over 10 acres. New modern toilet blocks, constant hot water, shop on site, tennis courts, basketball play area, launderette, food take-away in high season, organised card games in high season, pool room with table tennis, etc. There are washing/shower facilities for disabled visitors. Direct access to 14 miles of sandy beach (not for wheelchairs). Good bass fishing off the beach. Good base for touring. Children welcome, pets allowed with caravans/Dormobiles only. From only £6.50 per unit low season; Senior Citizens' reductions and reductions in May and September.

CAMPING SITES

KILMUCKRIDGE. 💬 🅰 **Morriscastle Strand Caravan and Camping Park, Kilmuckridge (05:**

30212, off season 01 535355; Fax: 01 545916). This site has been operated by the same family for 25 years, bu has been regularly refurbished and now caters for up to 10 touring vans, with pitches spread over 10 acres. New moder toilet blocks, constant hot water, shop on site, tennis courts basketball play area, launderette, food take-away in hig season, organised card games in high season, pool roo with table tennis, etc. There are washing/shower facilities fc disabled visitors. Direct access to 14 miles of sandy beac (not for wheelchairs). Good bass fishing off the beach. Goo base for touring. Children welcome, pets allowed wit caravans/Dormobiles only. From only £6.50 per unit lo season; Senior Citizens' reductions and reductions in Ma and September.

PUBLISHER'S NOTE

While every effort is made to ensure accuracy, we regret that FHG Publications cannot accept responsibility for errors, omissions or misrepresentation in our entries or any consequences thereof. Prices in particular should be checked because we go to press early. We will follow up complaints but cannot act as arbiters or agents for either party.

ONE FOR YOUR FRIEND 1994

FHG Publications have a large range of attractive holiday accommodation guides for all kinds of holiday opportunities throughout Britain. They also make useful gifts at any time of year. Our guides are available in most bookshops and larger newsagents but we will be happy to post you a copy direct if you have any difficulty. We will also post abroad but have to charge separately for post or freight.

The inclusive cost of posting and packing the guides to you or your friends in the UK is as follows:

Farm Holiday Guide ENGLAND, WALES and IRELAND
Board, Self-catering, Caravans/Camping, Activity Holidays. Over 400 pages. **£4.50**

Farm Holiday Guide SCOTLAND
All kinds of holiday accommodation. **£3.00**

SELF-CATERING & FURNISHED HOLIDAYS
Over 1000 addresses throughout for Self-catering and caravans in Britain. **£3.80**

BRITAIN'S BEST HOLIDAYS
A quick-reference general guide for all kinds of holidays. **£3.00**

The FHG Guide to CARAVAN & CAMPING HOLIDAYS
Caravans for hire, sites and holiday parks and centres. **£3.00**

BED AND BREAKFAST STOPS
Over 1000 friendly and comfortable overnight stops. Non-smoking, The Disabled and Special Diets Supplements. **£3.80**

CHILDREN WELCOME! FAMILY HOLIDAY GUIDE
Family holidays with details of amenities for children and babies. **£4.00**

Recommended SHORT BREAK HOLIDAYS IN BRITAIN
'Approved' accommodation for quality bargain breaks. Introduced by John Carter. **£4.00**

Recommended COUNTRY HOTELS OF BRITAIN
Including Country Houses, for the discriminating. **£4.00**

Recommended WAYSIDE INNS OF BRITAIN
Pubs, Inns and small hotels. **£4.00**

PGA GOLF GUIDE
Where to play and where to stay
Over 2000 golf courses in Britain with convenient accommodation. Endorsed by the PGA. Holiday Golf in France, Portugal and Majorca. **£8.50**

PETS WELCOME!
The unique guide for holidays for pet owners and their pets. **£4.50**

BED AND BREAKFAST IN BRITAIN
Over 1000 choices for touring and holidays throughout Britain. Airports and Ferries Supplement. **£3.00**

THE FRENCH FARM AND VILLAGE HOLIDAY GUIDE
The official guide to self-catering holidays in the 'Gîtes de France'. **£8.50**

Tick your choice and send your order and payment to FHG PUBLICATIONS, ABBEY MILL BUSINESS CENTRE, SEEDHILL, PAISLEY PA1 1TJ (TEL: 041-887 0428. FAX: 041-889 7204). **Deduct** 10% for 2/3 titles or copies; 20% for 4 or more.

Send to: NAME ....

ADDRESS ....

....

.... POST CODE ....

I enclose Cheque/Postal Order for £ ....

SIGNATURE .... DATE ....